Dear Bonnie !
Thank you for
motivation me today!

NOT JUST A
NUMBER

Enjoy my book !

xo Dorota xo

Dorota Nigro
with
Chris Moore

ACKNOWLEDGEMENTS

Not Just a Number was born from the pain, suffering, and anger I endured when my husband Anthony passed away after a brief battle with Stage IV lung cancer. The book was written not only as a tribute to my husband, but for his friends and coworkers at the MTA, who lost their lives just like he did, and from the same cause: diesel fumes. The measure of their lives should not be viewed in the number of years they lived, but rather in the love they left behind.

As I look back on the five years since my husband's death, I can't help but recall Anthony's friends who provided support and offered my family the comfort and hope we needed to keep going. Anthony was a devoted and loving husband and father who protected our family to the last minute of his life. He was not just a number to us, and neither are those people who helped me in the ensuing years. I am grateful to the TWU Local 100 members, both retired and active – those who want their names mentioned and those who do not out of fear of reprisals – for their support and never ending help, in person and through the *MaBSTOA Garages Then and Now* Facebook page. You provided me with tons of information, as well as testimony, and helped me to win the compensation case and ultimately encouraged me to write this book.

Without your help and sacrifice *Not Just a Number* would never have been written. THANK YOU!

My son Michael and my daughter Samantha also deserve a great deal of credit for listening to their mother and helping to support me, and by being the strong adult children any parent would be proud of. They believed in me, and in this project, in spite of all the time it took me away from them.

I am also grateful to my sister Urszula, who was always there for us no matter what; my two girlfriends Mary and Barbara and their families, who treated us like their own; James Dockerty, for keeping my husband's memory alive by constantly texting me and telling me Anthony's stories from work; Elwanda Stephens, for using her knowledge and union background to teach me how unions operate internally and for the long hours she spent reading early drafts and expressing her feelings about each chapter; Loretta Prino, who offered her comments and suggestions on the early drafts; all the flight attendants at United Airlines, my friends and coworkers, who listened to me for hours while sitting in the jump seat on flights to and from Delhi and Mumbai, India; my neighbors, who were always there when I needed them; Kathleen Coronia, a friend and good listener throughout the years; John Dearie, of the John Dearie Law Firm, who bravely fought and sadly lost a lawsuit on behalf of those of us adversely affected by diesel exhaust; and Brian O'Keefe and Alissa Gardos, who, along with the dedicated staff of the law firm Grey & Grey, won a compensation lawsuit on my behalf.

Special thanks to our editor Jeanie Karmiller, who helped us improve our manuscript by asking tough questions, and by honestly pointing out where we lacked for clarity and organization.

Last but not least, I should thank my coauthor, Chris Moore, whose ability to listen, commitment, and perseverance made the long hard task of writing a book a little easier. I'm happy that

Chris's father in-law thought so highly as to recommend him to a friend of mine who recommended him to me.

Life is full of strange coincidences that aren't always coincidental. Completing this book is one of those.

Anthony always believed that he was living out his destiny. I know completing this book and building an awareness of the historic dangers of diesel fumes is mine.

Dorota Nigro
September 2017

PROLOGUE

When he realized that I was planning to fight the MTA in court, Anthony turned to me from the passenger seat and said, "You'll never win! They have a legal department." We were on our way back from learning that his Stage IV lung cancer had been caused by the exposure to diesel fumes he had encountered while working for the MTA as a bus mechanic.

"It's not worth it, Dorota," he continued. "I'm just a number. Don't you get it! I'm just a number to them!"

I was floored and livid. He wasn't just a number to me, or to our children. I couldn't accept this view any more than I could accept that New York's Mass Transit Authority could expose its workers to toxic fumes in closed garages for decades, killing many of them, without repercussion.

I also knew that I wasn't the only woman in New York who had lost a loved one working for the MTA. Anthony attended funerals for so many current and former coworkers over the years that I had come to dread hearing news of another death. I am embarrassed to say, however, that in spite of all the funerals my husband attended, I never connected bus fumes to the relatively short lives of MTA employees, and had no idea that they were also killing my husband. It wasn't until this specific doctor's appointment, which came close to the end of Anthony's life, that I understood the reality of my husband's condition and where it came from.

After learning that diesel was the cause, I wasn't about to sit idly by and accept that the MTA had spent decades exposing Anthony to air they had to have known was making workers sick. I certainly hadn't fled Soviet-occupied Poland with my mother and sister to come to the land of opportunity – the land of the free and the brave — to have a major municipal transit company use my husband as if his life was expendable; the same way the Soviet communists used their own people.

I had already witnessed the ways in which a ruthless government could wield power over its citizens, and I couldn't stand to see an American company, a public-benefit corporation, no less, demonstrate such indifference to its workers' lives in my adopted homeland.

From that day forward, I vowed to fight to prove that the cancer that ultimately killed Anthony was caused by the diesel fumes he had inhaled on the job. Eventually, I would win the first legal victory in a workers' compensation court establishing the link between occupational diesel fume exposure and cancer.

My greatest hope is to open a larger national discussion about the historical dangers of diesel fumes, showing in what way these buses came to dominate public surface transportation in the first place, and how the companies involved valued their own bottom lines over the utility of service, air quality, and the lives of their employees. I also explain how a girl from Poland, one who has worked as a flight attendant for 33 years, came to win a landmark case in the United States regarding this multi-decade outrage.

CHAPTER 1

POLAND

I was born in Świebodzin, a small town in the western part of Poland, in 1955. Although WWII had ended 10 years previously, the country was still reeling from its effects. Poland had been occupied first by the Germans, and then the Russians; the two regimes together had killed approximately six-million Poles, the majority of whom were victims of war crimes and crimes against humanity.

Poland emerged from the war under the domination of the expanding U.S.S.R., and the de facto annexation of Poland by the Russians was formalized with the signing of the Warsaw Pact the year I was born.

Socialism controlled our lives. Despite Catholicism being almost universal in Poland, the church had little influence on my family or our neighbors. The Soviet Union remained the dominant economic and sociopolitical force, not only in Poland, but in our fellow Eastern Bloc countries as well. Our education emphasized friendship with Russia and included the recitation of poems about Lenin. Beginning in the fifth grade, our school children started learning Russian. This gradual indoctrination began early on and continued beyond high school to the extent that, while we all knew who Lenin was, few of us knew who the president of Poland was.

Despite the Soviet Union's obvious presence in our lives, we lived in a beautiful area of Poland and had a sense of security. Our quiet town of Świebodzin was located in a valley surrounded by small villages, farms, pine forests and lakes. It was so small that you could walk from one side of the town to the other in twenty minutes.

My grandparents owned a farm not far from Świebodzin in the small village of Pałck. I loved it there, and spent countless hours walking in the beautiful orchards and fields.

The story of our farm is worth recounting, as it reflects some elements that particularly came to characterize my life and gave me a perspective that was instrumental, decades later, in my decision to fight the MTA.

My grandfather, Franciszek, was born not far from Warsaw on September 17, 1892. His mother, Józefa Łominska, was a servant on a large farm. After becoming pregnant by the farm's owner, she remained there to raise her son; the boy who would become my grandfather. Józefa died during the First World War. After her death, my grandfather's father placed him into the elite, Pilsudski Army. Once he had completed his term, my grandfather was given a small farm in Ukraine by the Polish government. There he met my grandmother, Leontyna. They married and had three children together, one girl and two boys, of whom my father was the middle child.

They lived happily on a largely self-sufficient farm in Ukraine, but it wasn't to last.

With Lenin's death in the early 1920s, Stalin adopted a much more vicious policy toward the people of Ukraine, a policy that ultimately created a forced famine which brought the death of millions of Ukrainians. My family was spared the famine, but when the Soviets pushed into Polish lands during WWII, our farm in

Ukraine was taken away by the Russians and the entire family was shipped to Siberia, ostensibly due to my grandfather's former position in Pilsudski's army. The family then spent five years in the far, far east, which was no picnic to be sure, but it may have been preferable to the fate that awaited them under Stalin.

In Siberia, my grandfather worked at a lumber yard. There, he became good friends with the person in charge. And for reasons that aren't clear, this man helped the entire family escape by helping them to board a transportation train headed for the western part of Russia. Once they arrived in the west, they continued to Poland and further on toward the German border.

It was 1944, and the war was coming to a close, borders shifted, Ukraine became a full possession of Russia, and the western border of Poland moved west into former German territory. In turn, the German army and the Germans inhabiting the area, including the town of Świebodzin, fled over the shifting borders into their shrinking country, leaving everything they couldn't carry behind them.

As the new borders were established, and the Germans were expelled, the Polish government resettled the area with Poles. My grandparents were among those people granted farms in the village of Pałck which had been German.

When he entered their new house for the first time, my grandfather found it clean but full of furniture. The home was void of people, or it should have been. My grandfather quickly realized, however, that the table was set for four, and that the bowls contained soup. When he saw that, he searched the farm to see if any inhabitants remained. He found no one in the house, but as he entered one of the barns in the rear he learned that the family who had once lived there had in fact stayed behind. The parents and two grown children had committed suicide and were hanging from the rafters in the barn attic. Grandfather cut them down and buried them in the corner of the orchard. My grandmother planted sunflowers there and for many years kept the plot clear of forest litter and debris.

Much later, relatives from the deceased family came to our house and asked grandmother if she remembered the former inhabitants. She took them to where my grandfather had buried their bodies. When they saw the place, they asked her about the flowers and thanked her. My grandmother also wouldn't allow children to enter the area. As I spent time on the farm in the summers, we learned early that the gravesite was off limits to us. But we were always intrigued by it, and as we came to know the story, the gravesite became a marker of both Polish history and our family's story.

In those summers, my family left our apartment in Świebodzin and traveled the 16 kilometers by train or bus to the farm in Pałck, not very far in distance, but a whole world away from the small apartment we inhabited in that little town. The village itself was comprised of 72 homes of working farms. It was the perfect place to spend summers as a child.

My grandfather worked the eleven hectares of land (about 27 acres), mostly by himself, and grew rye, wheat, barley and potatoes. He worked it with a plow pulled by two horses. The farm also had two homes which needed to be maintained. In other words, my grandparents worked from sunup until sundown. While we were there, my parents helped as much as they could.

Everything we ate on the farm came from the land: vegetables, fruit, poultry, veal, pork and lamb, milk, eggs and cheese. My grandparents baked their own bread and sweet babka in the brick oven. They did it all by hard physical labor: planting vegetables, grains and raising pigs, sheep, geese, and chicken for meat. Cows supplied milk that we used to make butter, farmer's cheese, and yogurt.

Spring, summer, and early fall were busy times on the farm, as we needed to finish the harvest by the end of September. I remember the harvest most of all. When we brought the rye in from the fields with grandfather, he used to pull the wagon full of it with the same two horses he used to pull the plow. I loved sitting next to him on that wagon, seated high up on the pile of rye riding down the cobbled village lanes. We sat so high I pulled flowers and leaves from the trees above my head.

At times, Grandfather would tell me stories of the Katyn Massacre, when the Soviets took 4,000 Polish officers and intelligentsia out into the forest and shot them and buried them there. For years, the act was blamed on the Germans, but they always denied it.

"Why are you telling me this?" I remember asking.

"Because I want you to know that these things happened, and you will never see it in a book."

He wanted the truth of what happened to live on.

It's a funny thing about truth, it comes out eventually, and even a truth so deeply buried as Katyn, ultimately did come to light after forty-nine years in 1989.

With all the time I spent with my grandfather, I regret that I didn't spend much time with grandmother. She was always running in and out of the house taking care of the housework, while I spent as much of my day as possible outside. From cleaning, to laundry, to cooking, she did all the jobs by hand. Housework was every bit as difficult as the farm work was then. And she always had a dinner ready on the table on time for everyone, usually consisting of soup, meat, potatoes, and a vegetable. Our dessert was typically a compote made of fruit that we drank with dinner. Grandmother made it out of apples, plums or cherries, whichever fruit was in season at that time. It was certainly a better menu than we had in town.

My parents met in Świebodzin. My mother, Zenobia, had left Belarus, which was part of the Soviet Union, and came to the western part of Poland in search of her sister at the end of the war.

Her sister had previously fled Belarus with her husband and his mother. My mother went after them and found out they were in Germany where she got in touch with them. By that time my uncle was working on an American base, a position which later enabled him to move to the United States, to Englewood Cliffs, New Jersey. But my mother wouldn't follow them out of old Europe then. Instead, her sister got word to her not to come to Germany, but to remain behind and to go to school to be a midwife, which is what she did. The immediate post-war world was a fluid and confused time for everyone.

She finished college and was placed in the village of Skąpe, which stood some four kilometers from Pałck. There she had a house where she ran a kind of medical center to care for pregnant women and also to teach them how to take care of newborns. The clinic wasn't meant for delivering babies, but she delivered a lot of them there since the women typically waited until the last minute to come to her, and were too advanced to go to a hospital. On one occasion, she delivered a baby in an ambulance van. It was winter, and she knelt so long on that frozen metal floor that her knees never quite recovered. She also made house calls, bicycling from village to village to see her patients. This brought her into contact with many people and vastly expanded her social circle.

My father, Boleslaw, was working in Świebodzin when he met my mother. I was born in January of 1955 after they were married. My sister, Urszula, was born three years after me.

When we were on the farm in the summertime, my father commuted to Świebodzin by bus or motorcycle where he held a position in the socialist party. He had been recruited into this position when he was a young man. In fact, he had once set out to become a doctor, but got very sick and could not return to medical school and continue the education. Not long after he left school and had recovered, he met recruiters for the Communist Party who travelled from village to village in search of young men. They

promised him education and a good job. He saw it as an opportunity for a better life and joined.

Because both of my parents worked, they had to arrange child-
care for us. As it turned out, the people who lived in the other
half of our house, which was divided like a duplex, babysat us. On
occasion, our local parish priest, Father Kowalski, who lived next-
door, also watched us. I often walked with him to the church where
I helped him to prepare Holy Communion. He used to make the
hosts in the kitchen while I stood on a chair. "The whole ones go
in the jar," he said, "The broken ones you can have."

I loved to play hide and seek with him also. I later learned that
he passed away from cancer. That was the first time I had ever
heard of the deadly disease.

My family and I also took special trips to my father's work on
Thursdays where we watched movies broken into segments that
we viewed over the course of several weeks. This turned out to be
the only TV we ever saw because we didn't have a television of our
own in the apartment or on the farm. It wasn't until later that my
parents were able to buy their own television, which was a treat
even though it only showed two channels, Channel 1 and 2, which
played only Polish programs, of course.

I started school when I was seven years old, where I became an
A student and enjoyed sports very much. I graduated elementary
school with honors and was accepted to high school, which was
an important achievement for me because it was such an expec-
tation in my family. Only students with high grades, and those
who planned to go to college, were allowed into high school then.
There was also a technical school and a vocational school for those
with different interests or lower grades. However, the students who
graduated from the technical school could continue their education in college, while the graduates of the vocational school were
given jobs in the town or had to seek employment in neighboring
areas.

I spent two years in that high school before we had to move to America. At the time, I was on a path, set by my parents, to prepare for medical school. My parents further made me take English, but I had a hard time with it, because I was already studying Russian and German.

"What do I need English for?" I said. "I will never use the stupid language as long as I live."

Despite my objections, and at my mother's insistence, I continued taking the language. While I had no knowledge of this at the time, of course, it would turn out to be fortunate for me, given the nature of upcoming events and the ways in which they changed my life forever. While I was in seventh grade, my father returned to college, as further education was important when seeking a better position in the government. It was part of the deal he had made with the Communist Party. He attended school an hour away from Świebodzin in Wrocław. It was too far for him to commute so he lived in Wrocław and used to visit us on the weekends. At the time my mother worked two jobs, one in the local hospital and the other in the high school, as a nurse.

After my father returned from college, my parents got a new apartment on the other side of town. It was a three room place on the second floor with running cold water. For hot water, we had to heat the water on top of the coal-fired cook-stove in the kitchen, including bathwater.

Even after my father returned from college and took work in Świebodzin, he was never home. He left early in the mornings and came back late at night. He was a Secretary of Agriculture for our community, and worked in the Communist Party building. This was the era of collective farming, and the produce of the farms was considered "government property." It was an influential position, and he stood in charge of the produce from several local villages, which made him well known among the people and farmers.

He was, unfortunately, also becoming well known for something else and began to get a reputation as a "ladies' man." At first the talk seemed to my mother to be a rumor, and my mother didn't appreciate gossip. But as time wore on, the gossips weren't simply gossips anymore.

The rumor was that my father, along with others, were using their position in the communist government to host parties with young ladies. When my mother caught wind of what was happening she exposed these events. I was only about twelve years old when it happened and I'm not clear on the details. This was a country where people had very little, especially when compared to Western countries. And since commerce and the economy were organized through the government, Communist Party officials were the real seats of power in every area. Using their muscle to have parties, which happened all over the Soviet countries to a greater or lesser degree, was a cause of great scandal, especially in our small community.

When my mother made it public, my father and the other men involved all lost their positions. And while they lost their positions, they weren't fired; that's not the way collectivist organizations operate. They just moved all the men into different positions in the county, my father included.

About two years after the scandal broke and they were divorced, my mother took us out of the country. I know that at the time my father was giving her difficulties as far as the child support and alimony were concerned.

She confided this in her sister, who had come to America ahead of her. My aunt and her husband had no children of their own and were willing to bring the three of us to the States to give us what my mother hoped would be a better life and to introduce to the American Dream.

CHAPTER 2

AMERICAN DREAM

My father fought my mother over child support after their divorce. Judging by the papers I found years later, the fight was uglier than I could have imagined. He pushed her to the point where she decided that she wanted to leave the country; a decision that changed my life and my sister's life forever.

My aunt and her husband already lived in the United States and my mother saw this as an opportunity to escape an unbearable situation for greener pastures across the ocean. It took almost a year after my mother began making efforts to leave Poland that all of our paperwork was processed by the Polish government to let us go, and by the Americans to accept us.

My father was the last obstacle; he needed to sign the paperwork to make it official, as both my sister Urszula and I were minors. I was on the verge of eighteen then, but my sister was three years younger than I, which meant she wouldn't be able to go without his consent.

He told my mother then that he needed to talk with me before he signed, and so I went to visit him in town. He was pleasant at first, but then he said, "You know that I don't have to let you go?"

"Yes, I do know that." I said. "You don't have to let me go, but I'll be 18 in two months. Then, I can do what I want. So, if you won't sign the papers now, it won't stop me. It will only affect Urszula, who will need to stay in Poland while we go to America."

I also believed that, in spite of what he was saying, that he would ultimately let us go. It was because of something I knew. On one occasion years before, my mother had gotten sick and had gone to the hospital for two days by herself. When she did that my father saw fit to bring the neighbor lady home with him in the middle of the night while we were sleeping.

We lived in a small, three-room apartment then. My sister and I slept in the bedroom, which was adjacent to the living room where my mother and father usually slept. The door between the rooms had an interesting feature: you couldn't open it without the hinge making a screeching sound that was audible throughout the entire apartment. On that night, I woke to go to the bathroom, and when I walked out of the bedroom, I caught him cheating. When I saw that, I turned back around and closed the door, but he knew I caught him, because the noise the door made was impossible not to hear. He never said anything, and I never said anything to my mother, or to anyone else for that matter, but he and I both knew.

"I think you will sign the papers," I said. "Because this is all your fault and you know it. I know that you know what I saw that night. Are you going to make it difficult for us again?"

He signed the papers shortly afterward. Very little could stop us now from leaving Poland. My mother had acquired five-year visas. When those five years were up we could choose to stay and become American citizens or not. We just had to finalize the visas at the American Consulate in Warsaw before we could go. I remember Nixon was elected President of the United States while we were there. They showed some of the proceedings on the old television in the consulate.

In the course of finalizing the visas, consulate staff asked my sister and me to sign a series of papers. I remember the consul general handed us one particular paper in an almost uncomfortable way. "Sign this," he said.

"What is it?" I asked. The man didn't answer. "Well, I don't want to sign it if I don't know what it is." I said.

"It's a document that states you won't practice prostitution while you're with us."

"What is this, something you make money on?"

"Dorota, just sign the paper!" my mother said and smiled at the man uncomfortably. I did what she told me, and we were given our visas.

From that point forward, nothing was going to stop us from going to America. The day came, and we took the train to Warsaw where we flew out of the country on KLM, Royal Dutch Airlines. Later, when we were married, my husband, Anthony, used to joke that I was "fresh off the boat." He'd also say I married him for a green card. Neither of those things were true. I had a visa and citizenship long before I met him. I also flew to the United States. I didn't take a boat.

"No," I'd respond to him. "I came on a royal airline, and you married me for the flight benefits." At that point, I was working as a flight attendant and he could fly for free, which he took full advantage of, but that was in the future.

We arrived in New York City on November 29th, 1972 after an entire year preparing the paperwork. I'll never forget the day we landed at John F. Kennedy Airport in Queens. As we approached the city, I saw the lights that looked green on the river in the distance, outlining the shape of the George Washington Bridge. I had never seen such a large structure before, and aside from that, the view of the city itself was breathtaking. There were so many lights, both in the city and up and down the coast. How many people lived here? Coming from Świebodzin, arriving in New York City was like traveling to another planet.

From JFK, we traveled an hour to the north and west, to my aunt and uncle's house in Dumont, New Jersey. The house was in a nice neighborhood within walking distance of the elementary school and high school.

The house they lived in was a half-Tudor. The entryway opened into a huge living room with a large fireplace, an adjacent dining room, kitchen and two bedrooms. Downstairs the entire basement was finished. That's where my sister and I slept, while my mother slept upstairs in the extra bedroom.

When we first arrived in America, my aunt took my mother to Sport Craft company in Bergenfield, New Jersey, where she got a job packing sporting equipment on the assembly line; the goods arrived from China and were distributed throughout the states.

The transition was tough for all of us, but I was young, and knew some English, so it wasn't so difficult for me. On the other hand, my mother had a hard time communicating with people. After all, she had spoken Polish her entire life. She didn't enjoy the type of work she needed to do either. She missed her home, the customs, the country, and the small town, and she needed a car but didn't drive. Those five years were very hard for her, and she also knew her salary wasn't nearly enough to give us the things we needed here.

My aunt worked nights so we didn't see her that often. I think she didn't want to be around with all those people in the house; it was too much work. However, we did see my uncle quite a bit, and over the course of the next few years, he became more like a father to me. He used to take me out to the mall and to other places. We had adventures together.

I remember the first time he took me to the Macy's in the Paramus Park Shopping Mall. We had nothing like this back home. First off, I was shocked just by the variety of stores they had in the mall. Then we went inside the Macy's Department Store, which was like a wonderland for me. America was such a beautiful and rich land. Clothing stores in Poland were in black and white compared to the vibrancy here where everything was bright and colorful. What impressed me as much as anything was that they

Dorota Nigro with Chris Moore

had my size in stock. I wore a size 4 or 6 petite. We could never find that in Poland. Whatever clothing we did get from the store my mother always had to alter. Macy's also gave me my first credit card, which I still have. I've had it since I was eighteen. Needless to say, in a short period of time with that card, I had shoes in every possible color. The shopping here helped to form my impression of this country.

I found Macy's a bit funny too, because the women's department seemed to comprise an entire floor, while the men's department was shunted all the way back in the corner and carried clothes that might have been in a store back in Poland for the bland and bleak coloring. I used to laugh with my uncle about it.

I fell in love with pizza then too. My uncle used to leave the house to buy a paper on the weekends. One time he asked if I wanted to come with him. I did. When he went inside the store to get his paper I noticed a sign outside on another store front that read, "pizza."

"What's that," I asked?

"What, pizza, you want to try it?"

I loved it. After that, my uncle took me to get pizza every Sunday. After a while, he started to joke, "I don't know if I can handle driving you here for another Sunday. You better marry an Italian who owns a pizza place."

Well, I married an Italian, but he didn't own a pizza place.

I started my American education at Dumont High. Early on, they tested me to see where I'd fit, starting with math, which as it turned out, I was advanced in. But as the only foreign student in high school, I had my own English teacher. Mr. Stark spent one hour each day with me walking around the school property and practicing English vocabulary. I was a very lucky eighteen-year-old to have my own English teacher. What Mr. Stark didn't know was that I had already had English lessons in Poland. I didn't bother to explain it to him. Why should I?

14

In Dumont, I now took advantage of the situation by not disclosing the fact that I knew enough English to know what was going on around me. I communicated through Mr. Halk, the school's Russian teacher, who also didn't know that I spoke some English. But my little game ended not long after I started there.

One day, Mr. Stark tested my English vocabulary. In the course of this he pointed to different objects around the room and made me name them in English. I think he was starting to guess that I knew more than I was letting on. I was also getting sick of playing stupid. He pointed to the water coming out of the water fountain and said, "What is it?"

I responded, "Beer."

We both started laughing. He realized at that moment that every day for two months I had been having fun with him. He wasn't mad, however.

I went straight into regular English class after that.

In January, I turned eighteen and my uncle began teaching me how to drive his car. If I was going to live here, then I had to learn. Very few people drove cars in Poland, they were too expensive. In fact, there was a lottery people had to sign up for just to get one. Well, in Jersey things were very different: having a car was a necessity as I would learn.

At the end of that school year, I graduated from Dumont High. After high school, I attended Bergen County Community College, where I took mainly English as Second Language (ESL) classes. I was surrounded by Spanish speaking students. I even took one semester of Spanish in order to understand and to fit in. But I soon realized that I needed more than Bergen County could offer me, and transferred to Montclair State where I majored in German and minored in Russian.

At Montclair, I had one of the most enjoyable experiences of my life. During that time, I also met, and became close friends with, another student. Mary McDonough and I first bonded while studying German together, and have become lifelong friends. She was a student at Montclair and majored in Spanish, and also in German like me. We spent a lot of time together.

In my second year at Montclair, I signed up for the study abroad program that sent us to Germany for the entire year. I had originally signed up to go to Munich. But after I met Mary I learned that she was also traveling to Germany, but in the part of the program that travelled to Konstanz, instead of to Munich, which was in effect the same trip, but two-thousand dollars cheaper. When I heard I could save that much money, I switched programs.

Dr. Moore, Director of the Foreign Languages Department at the time, thought that my going to Germany was a bad idea.

"You need to practice your English, Miss Sowinska," he said. "Now is not the time to get better at another language." Well, I went anyway, in spite of what he had said. As it turned out, traveling to a foreign country with twenty-two native English speakers was the best thing I could have done for my English.

At home in New Jersey, I lived in a Polish household, which meant I didn't have to speak English except when I was in school. But in the program, I was forced to speak in either German or English, because no one would have understood me otherwise. Being forced to speak in either of those non-native languages helped me get a much stronger hold on both. It probably was the best decision I ever made to improve my English, not to mention the highlight of my time in school.

While we were in Europe, I planned to spend Christmas in Poland with my family. I invited Mary along because I knew that it was going to be too expensive for her to fly back to the states. Inviting her seemed so innocent; it would, however, set the stage for an adventure that would introduce Mary to the way the world worked behind the Iron Curtain. We bought train tickets headed for Poland in Stuttgart, Germany. From there, we rode the train for 18 hours, changing trains at least once, before we finally arrived in West Berlin, which at the time was divided from the east, and from the rest of western Germany for that matter.

In Berlin, there was a line demarcating West from East which we stood beside and put our legs across. Above us, two young soldiers held machine guns and watched our antics without smiling. We could see them looking at us, but we didn't mind.

When you're young, you're really stupid.

Finally, our train pulled up and I started panicking. The train we had tickets for turned out to be a Russian train. You could see the Cyrillic writing on the side and white curtains and Russian people inside. I knew that such trains didn't stop in small towns. In fact, this particular train only made four stops: Paris, Berlin, Warsaw, and Moscow. I thought they must have sold us the wrong tickets at that point. But it turned out I had the correct ticket, at least the only ticket for a train bound for Poland, yet it was strictly for Russian citizens.

"What are we going to do now?" Mary asked.

"We're getting on it anyway!" I said. At that point, we attempted to enter the train, and just pretended as though we didn't know we had tickets that were only issued to Russians. After viewing our passports, however, the conductor said, "You can't get on this train." I started arguing with him in Russian. I told him that I had to be home for Christmas, and that we had bought the tickets in Stuttgart without any trouble. By this point, all the Russians on the train started looking out the windows to see what the trouble was.

Two young Russians then came down off the train and talked the conductor into letting us on, which we were grateful for.

The train was beautiful. All red carpeting, and white curtains with Russian teapots, known as samovars, in each and every car. But as the train left the station, Mary started freaking out and wondering what she was going to write to her parents to tell them she was never coming home again. She said she thought she was on her way to Siberia.

Some of the Russians on the train started asking me if there was anything wrong with my girlfriend. "She's fine," I said, "she's American."

The train ride was an hour and a half long. It was two o'clock in the morning when we arrived at the Świebodzin train station, but we were in for a surprise. I knew that Świebodzin wasn't technically a stop this train made, but I thought they would make an exception since they let us on the train. I was wrong, they weren't going to stop, and yet they still intended to have us get off at the correct station.

The procedure for our disembarking was as follows. The platform was as dark as can be with maybe one or two lights. The train proceeded slowly through the station where it was supposed to be speeding. Beyond the station the train then slowed even further for our sake, and at that point, the same two Russian men who had argued for our entry onto the train now helped us off, carrying our suitcases. We hesitated for a moment and then, with the help of the two Russians, jumped off the slow-moving train onto the gravel road base and railroad ties without too much trouble. The kind men then turned and quickly climbed back onto the train and, with several others, waved goodbye as they disappeared into the night.

"This is crazy," Mary said.

"We better get off the tracks," I said, and we climbed through some nearby bushes and walked to my family's apartment.

The November after I returned from Germany marked the five-year anniversary of my family coming to America, which meant that we had to choose whether or not to remain Americans as per our visas. My mother did not want to remain in the United States, and so, after my sister, Urszula, graduated high school, they both went back to Poland, where Urszula was admitted into medical school. What happened to her then says a lot about American education.

Urszula had the grades in the United States to go to a Polish medical school, but she learned when she arrived that she was behind the other students and eventually dropped out. You might say that she wasn't meant for medical school, but I know that had she completed high school in Poland, she would have been prepared.

As for me, I wasn't going to bother going back to Poland at all, my first trip to Macy's had sealed the deal. I loved the United States.

In order to become a citizen when the five years were up, you had to go before a judge who gave you a little quiz. If you passed the quiz, then he would sign your papers and that was that. Well, I waited in this line to get my quiz from the judge. I thought that it might be difficult and secret. But as I waited, I heard the judge ask every candidate the same question over and over, "Who was the first President?"

The answer would come back, "George Washington." Even if you didn't know who the first president was, by the time you got up to the front of the line, unless you were deaf or didn't speak a word of English, then you knew.

I had taken the time to study for the quiz, so I was a little put off that it was more like a rubber stamp than anything else. I thought I'd feel embarrassed if that was the question he asked me to pass the test, and so when I got to the front of the line I said, "Please don't ask me the same question. Can you ask me something else?" He smiled at me when I said that.

"Why do you want to be an American?" he said. He had also asked this question of some of the other candidates, who started telling a sob story, and lying, "Oh, I had to escape socialism," or they'd say some other such thing. I wasn't going to say any of that. I decided to tell the truth.

When the judge asked me why I wanted to be an American I said, "Macy's."

"Macy's?" he said.

"Yeah. I came here five years ago and saw Macy's for the first time. After that I never wanted to go back."

"Ok, here you are. Congratulations, you're an American. Sign the papers."

I signed the papers and walked out of the courtroom an American.

On the way out, I learned all about the two-party system. After leaving the judge's chambers, all the new Americans passed through the same set of doors and into a hallway where there were two tables set up, one on the left and one on the right. If you were going to exit the building you turned to the left, where the Republicans had their table set up. I didn't know much about politics, but I do know that everyone I saw exit signed up as a Republican that day. And so I was a Republican for a little while. I later became a Democrat. I'm not a member of either party anymore.

As a freshly minted American, and after three years at Montclair, including one year in Germany, I graduated with a degree in education, and started working as a teacher.

Since she had majored in both German and Spanish, Mary got a job teaching Spanish at the Wall High School. I followed her there and became the German and Russian teacher shortly after that. But it was hard to make ends meet on that salary, which is a shame since teaching is the most important profession there is. I had to look elsewhere for part-time work, and started working as a cocktail waitress on the weekends where I made more money in ten hours than in 40 hours teaching. Then my friend, Steve Humanik, told me about a new airline company, called People Express, that was looking for flight attendants. The company paid very well and was looking for young, multilingual applicants with teaching backgrounds and work experience. They may as well have put my name on the job application. I was also attracted to the job for other reasons: when I was a little girl in Poland I used to look up at the sky when the planes flew over and imagine what it would be like to be a stewardess. Now I would know.

Steve introduced me to the company and set me up with a final board interview, allowing me to skip some of the process. He said that I would be great at the job because of my knowledge of foreign languages.

I arrived at the office where the interview was to be conducted. The four-person board called me into the room. Inside, I found a single chair before the table where they sat waiting for me.

They asked me to take a seat. I did so, but I didn't know that the chair was on wheels. Maybe the chair was a bit higher than I anticipated. Whatever it was, when I sat back, the chair rolled away with me on it and crashed into the rear wall. The interviewers looked shocked. One of them stood up. Before anyone could speak, I crossed my legs and said, "Now I am ready!"

With that the interview began. I was hopeful that I did well. When they finished, they asked me to step out of the room, but I hadn't even touched the door handle when they called me back.

I was hired, and I've been working in the industry ever since.

I also got a $30,000 pay increase in one afternoon.

CHAPTER 3

SKI HOUSE

Mary and her friends used to rent a ski house on Hunter Mountain in Upstate New York every ski season. Her friend Dennis would rent the house next door with a group of friends and fellow firemen from New York City. One year, they decided to share a house and eliminate the cost of a second rental.

In ten years of Mary renting that place, I had only gone up twice. I didn't ski. But Mary had insisted this year, and so I planned to go.

I was exhausted when I pulled up in front of Mary's house from Newark International Airport that Friday afternoon fresh off a four-day trip. And I almost choked when I saw all the stuff Mary had piled on the curb, and which she expected me to fit in my car: pillows, blankets, a toaster, pots, pans, utensils. I just pulled up, said, "Hello," and walked right into the house to change out of my uniform and into jeans. I couldn't deal with trying to fit all that into my new Buick Skylark.

By the time I came out from my shower, she had us ready to leave. "You drive," I said. "I haven't slept since yesterday," and I got into the car and reclined in the passenger seat, took a pillow and blanket, and slept for the entire four-hour drive to the Catskills. Mary didn't care if I slept or not. She was just happy to have me go.

The way this trip worked was that the guys typically came and skied during the week, while the girls went up for a long weekend. But on this particular occasion, the two groups ran a kind of open house where everybody came together to start the season. While I went up Friday with Mary, some of the guys showed up the next day, which happened to be Saturday, the 15th of November, 1986.

We woke up that Saturday morning and started drinking mimosas for breakfast. It was still early in the season, so I don't think we planned on doing much skiing. We were up just to have a vacation, which meant we weren't all that motivated to leave the house early.

I remember that I was sitting in a chair on the side of the room opposite the front door that afternoon when Dennis came in with Anthony. When I saw him, I felt a strong connection between us. I had more than just a sense about Anthony. I thought, "Oh my God, I'm going to marry that guy."

When I thought that, I remember talking myself down. "Ok, Dorota," I said to myself. "I know you had a couple mimosas, but you're not drunk. Don't jump so far ahead." Even with the pep-talk, I still had this feeling that told me he was the one.

Why? As much as I can explain, I always knew I needed to be with someone as strong as I am or stronger. I would have just pushed somebody with a weaker personality around.

I certainly felt a strong personality when I laid eyes on Anthony. It wasn't that he was Mister America, but a normal guy, a strong man, a kind man, and some other innate traits that aren't easy to put in words. He could also talk.

I watched as Mary approached the guys to say hello. Then she looked back at me and said, "I want you to meet my girlfriend, Dorota." With that, they walked toward me. Anthony and Dennis said, "Hello," but Anthony decided to sit down in a chair next to mine.

I felt comfortable with him immediately. And he must have felt comfortable with me too, because we stayed there, talking, for the rest of the afternoon.

Anthony didn't mention it at first, but I was shaking his chair without thinking about it while he was talking. He sat to my left, and I had put my foot on the piece of wood down by the floor that connected the two legs of his chair and was nervously shaking my leg. Eventually, after I guess he couldn't pretend that he didn't notice the shaking anymore, he mentioned it, "Is something wrong with you? Are you nervous?" he asked.

I couldn't believe he asked me that. "I have a feeling that makes me nervous. That's all." I responded.

"A feeling? What feeling's that?"

"I have a feeling we're going to date each other, and that scares the heck out of me." Actually, I had a feeling we were going to marry, but I couldn't tell him that right away. Then he really might have run off. As it stood, he looked up at the door leading to the kitchen as if he needed an escape.

"Excuse me," he said, "I need a drink," and then he got up and left. As he turned to go, he asked if I wanted anything. I replied "No," since he seemed to ask that question out of courtesy. But to my surprise, he returned a few minutes later with a drink and a small plate of food.

"Would you like some?" he said, holding out his plate in my direction. From there, we kept on talking, while he ignored the whole comment I'd made about dating and went on to tell me about his parents and brothers and about his life in general. Anthony did most of the talking, which he wasn't shy about doing. It was obvious that we were both comfortable with each other.

I found out that he was of Italian descent. Both his parents were born in the United States, but his grandparents came "on the boat," his grandfather from Naples and his grandmother from the Bari region of Italy. He was one of three sons, the middle child. His father worked for a printing company. His Mother was a secretary, but when she gave birth to their first son, Joseph, she stayed home and took care of the family. Originally, they had lived in Brooklyn, but his parents decided to move to New Hyde Park in Long Island when Anthony was thirteen years old. They bought a house there where Anthony and his brothers attended Catholic elementary and high schools.

Anthony displayed a natural talent for fixing things from childhood. He loved cars, and after college became a car mechanic, landing a few jobs early with local car dealerships. He finally got a big job with the Mass Transit Authority of New York City (MTA) in 1983; that's the company that runs the subways, buses and rails in New York City. Anthony's move from small, local car dealerships to the MTA was a big step up in the world. The job offered better pay, a pension, medical and vision coverage. The job also offered flexible hours because it allowed Anthony to pick certain jobs in various depots, which in the future would enable him to work with and around my schedule, which was also flexible.

The MTA position, unfortunately, also offered something I was unaware of: exposure to diesel fumes on a daily basis. But such a thought was far from my mind on our first encounter on Hunter Mountain.

He and I talked until dark that evening, and then everyone else got ready to leave to go to a local bar. Anthony and I followed. But at the bar we got separated in the crowd and noise. I relocated Anthony after a few minutes, and when I did, I began to fear that he had his eyes on Roberta, the blond bombshell from our group. But when one of the guys kept hitting on me (incidentally, he was Polish, and thought that fact entitled him to make a move on me), I took the opportunity to escape him by pulling Anthony onto the dance floor. While the Polish guy got the hint, the move also gave

Anthony and me our first dance. The DJ, to my surprise, played a slow song, and as we danced close together, I felt the same as I had when he first walked through the door. I felt like this was *it.* I was at home in his arms.

The next morning, I was in the living room sipping coffee when Anthony walked in and sat next to me. He carried a Wall Street Journal in one hand and a cup of coffee in the other. We talked for few minutes, and then he asked for my phone number. "Yes." I said.

After he wrote it down, I said, "Well, give me your number in case I'm delayed when you call, this way I can reach you." At that time, getting a phone call wasn't as easy as it is today when everyone has cell phones at all times. Then, you actually had to be near to a land line, which could be difficult for a flight attendant.

He agreed to give me his number, but when he began to write it on the newspaper, it seemed like he was having trouble remembering his own area code. He tried three times to write his phone number. I watched as he wrote "212;" then crossed that out and wrote "718;" then he crossed that number out and wrote "516." When I saw him do all that, I said, "Listen I might be Polish, but I'm not stupid. I don't need your number. When you call me, and I'm home, we can go out. If you don't, no problem, but don't insult me by trying to give me the wrong area code. I will not call you."

"Oh no," he said, "Here it is," and he handed me a piece of paper with his correct phone number on it this time. I took it from him and put it in my pocket. I don't know what he was thinking with those area codes.

The girls left Hunter Mountain early the next morning. All of us had long rides to either Jersey or Long Island to look forward to. During the trip home, I couldn't shake the sense that my time with Anthony on the mountain was merely the beginning of something that would significantly alter both our lives.

Despite the fact that he had waffled when I asked him for his number, I wasn't surprised when Anthony called me a few days later asking for a date. That weekend, he drove his old Chrysler Córdoba to my apartment in Jersey for dinner. The only trouble was that I wasn't there. I was late.

I was originally supposed to cook for Anthony, but my flight was delayed. I couldn't get home on time, and since I couldn't call to let him know, as he was coming over from Long Island, he just had to wait for me. When I got home late, I still had to stop at a store to pick up groceries to make dinner. I was totally unprepared and rushing around. I recall that I bought chicken cutlets and steak because I wasn't sure what my plan was. On top of that, I also got a ton of appetizers including cheese, crackers, and grapes.

The weather was just awful too, and as I approached I saw Anthony waiting for me in the rain.

"I'm sorry," I said when he helped me out of the car. "We got delayed." It had rained all day long and my uniform was wet and my hair was a mess. I was in no shape to go out on a date or to even have him see me. I wasn't a pretty picture. That much was evident. But he behaved like a gentleman and helped me with my groceries.

Inside he said, "Why don't you change your clothes, and we'll go out to dinner? I'll wait."

Thank God he said that.

We had a great dinner and then stayed at the restaurant for hours, just talking and enjoying each other's company. The connection between us was obvious. Not to repeat myself, but I felt like I was at home with him. And he must have had something of the same feeling since he set up another date for the following weekend. This time I made the trip to Long Island to see him. It was a long drive out to the house where he lived with his brother in Williston Park, two hours or so, and I was afraid of getting lost the entire time, but I was determined to get there because I knew that we would end up together.

When I successfully arrived at his house, he took me to the Swiss Chalet restaurant in Rosslyn on the North Shore of Long Island. The food was great. Again, we both felt comfortable talking with each other and just enjoying the company. Then Anthony turned the entire date on its head when he brought up what I had said at Hunter Mountain a few weeks prior. Up until that point he had acted like he had forgotten about it. "Do you still think we are going to date?" he said; then he added, "Is it going to be a serious relationship?"

I waited for a moment to respond, but I felt like I needed to correct what he said. "Well, we are already dating, but the feeling I had wasn't actually that we are going to date," I paused at that point and then said. "It was a strong feeling that we will get married. That's what was making me nervous."

"Married!"

"I'm 99% sure."

"What about the other 1%?"

"It all depends on your mother."

"What does my mother have to do with our marriage?"

"I will never marry a man if I have to go through life knowing that his mother doesn't like me."

We moved off the subject then and finished dinner, but what I said must have stuck with him because not long after that Anthony excused himself from the table for a moment. When he returned he paid the bill.

"Let's have coffee and dessert somewhere else," he said in an almost absent way. I was beginning to wonder if I had made a mistake in telling him I had a feeling we would marry.

We left the Swiss Chalet and began driving. He didn't mention the destination. We drove for a while; at some point, I noticed that we had entered a residential neighborhood. I couldn't imagine where he was taking me. Shortly afterward, Anthony pulled up in front of a private home.

"What are we doing? Where's dessert?" I said.

"Giving you the chance to see if it's 100%."

It became clear now that our arrival at this location wasn't a surprise to anyone but me. As the front door opened, his mother came out and walked toward us with a smile on her face. He must have called them from the restaurant when he left the table before he paid the bill.

At that point, Anthony let me out of the car. I walked toward his mother, who was fast closing the distance and said, "Hello." She came right up to me, smiled, and gave me a hug, but more than a regular hug it was like she was holding onto me. She even gave me a kiss.

I don't think he brought many girls home to meet his mother, and he was a thirty-one-year-old man at that point, so his mother knew what it meant when he brought me home. She obviously wanted me to know that she accepted me with open arms. Not bad for a girl who came over on a royal airline from behind the Iron Curtain.

When she let go, I looked over my shoulder and said to Anthony, who was standing behind us, "It's 100%."

In March of 1987 we moved in together.

Mary reminds me that when she found out that we had moved in together she complained that she had been renting the place for ten years at Hunter Mountain and still hadn't found a man, "and you come up once and find a husband." She swears that I replied, "Well, that's because you call it 'Hunt-Her' Mountain. I call it 'Hunt-Him'.

I probably said it. I know that when Anthony asked me to move in with him, I nodded and said, "There are few things we need to do first. But the most important is that you need to tell your mother that I am moving in with you. You are telling her too, not asking her. My parents are not here, so it doesn't bother them, but I don't want your Italian mother to hear it through the grapevine that we're going to live together."

It took me two months to move in with Anthony. I remember the day when we drove from Jersey to Long Island together with my Queen-size mattress strapped to the top of my brand-new Buick Skylark. I worried it would scratch the roof. I loved Buicks then. I suppose because of my uncle.

After we moved in, Anthony's mother didn't wait long to pressure him into marrying me. His mother did all the work. I just let the chips fall into place.

He proposed to me over a steak dinner in his apartment watching "Who's the Boss." I used to love that show. He said, "Would you like to marry me," and opened the little box with the ring in it.

"What? You're proposing here watching my favorite show?" Then I said "Yes" without hesitation.

After he proposed to me, both his mother, Marie, and his Father, Joseph, took me to Kleinfeld in Brooklyn to look at wedding dresses. I went in with a clipping of a dress in my wallet. It was just perfect, but when the saleswoman brought the dress out for me to try on, I knew it was all wrong as soon as I laid eyes on it. That dress must have been made for a woman over six feet tall. There was no way it was going to fit me. I felt a bit dejected.

I must have looked upset because the saleswoman said, "Don't worry, I have the perfect dress."

She brought out the new one. I put it on in the dressing room, and it fit perfectly. To my surprise, it didn't need a single alteration. Kleinfeld was a long way from those barren shops in Poland I'd been to with my mother where nothing ever fit me because I was too petite.

When I returned from the dressing room in that dress, my mother-in-law, with tears in her eyes, said, "You look beautiful."

After buying the perfect dress was out of the way, planning for our wedding began in earnest. Anthony and I intended to get married in a Catholic Church. This posed a potential problem, however, since I had never made my first communion. I had, in fact, been Christened, but even that was done with a bit of secrecy. Poland was a communist country and my father was a member of the Communist Party, which was vehemently atheist. This meant that children of party members were typically not baptized or allowed to attend church, but, for my mother, having me Christened was important. Since she worked in the hospital, she chose one of the doctors as my godfather, the nurse as godmother, and a priest quietly completed the ceremony in a matter of minutes not long after I was born. After that, however, religious education, communion, and confirmation had been out of the question. This is the way things worked for a lot of Poles then, but mostly for the ones who were in the Communist Party, before democracy came and the church turned into big business.

We did attend church from time to time, however, but only sporadically and only during holidays when I was growing up, and typically with my grandparents. I recall that we spent Christmas and Easter with them on the farm. My grandparents were very religious. They attended church every Sunday. I can still remember entering that tiny church in the village at Christmas-time, which was decorated beautifully inside with a full-sized, real pine tree and hundreds of candles surrounding it. The atmosphere had a strong aura of mystery to it. While the temperature inside the church was freezing, the people were warm, the feeling was warm, and it was beautiful. Maybe I'll be able to see that type of Christmas celebration again someday.

If I wanted to be married in the Catholic Church in Long Island, however, I needed to solve my problem, and so I entered the Floral Park church's rectory and spoke with the priest there, Father Francis. I explained my situation to him. He was very understanding. Father Francis told me not to worry about it. He said he would take care of it, and he did. I received my First Communion on the day of our wedding and was confirmed by the Bishop of Rockville Center later that day. He entered St. Hedwig's church on my wedding day and said, "I guess you're the Polish girl getting married."

I smiled.

We had the ceremony in both languages; that is, in both English and Polish, and my parents came from Poland together for the event.

Our reception took place at Crest Hollow Country Club in Woodberry, Long Island. It was October, 16th 1987. Now we were married and happy, but there was something else to come – a dream – in fact, two dreams that would remain with me until this day.

Anthony owned a house with his older brother, Joey, on Van Wagner Place in Williston Park. We decided to live there after our wedding and planned to build an extension onto the house for us to live in. But I got pregnant before we had the chance of adding on, and, as the baby developed, we learned that he would have a congenital heart defect. It's heartbreaking news to receive when you're pregnant, and especially when it's your first child, because you already don't know what to expect. You're afraid of what might go wrong; or, you're afraid that you won't do the right thing with your diet or with any number of things pertaining to your body and health, and when you actually learn that something is wrong, it confirms the underlying dread.

But before he was born, and after we knew he had the problem, I had two vivid dreams.

In the first, I dreamt of a white porcelain box. I could see that box so clearly, but the corner of it was broken and my wedding dress was exposed there on the inside, yet the dress wasn't white; it was midnight black. That dream of the white box with the black dress scared me badly before the birth and stayed with me like a shadow.

There was no time to dwell on these things. However, I did tell my mother about the dream. She had come in from Poland because she knew the baby was sick. I also told Anthony. I don't think either had much to say.

Then I delivered the child on June 13th, 1989. He was delivered through C-section at the doctor's recommendation so as not to put him through the additional stress of a live birth, further taxing his already weakened system.

The doctors weren't alarmed with his condition immediately when he was born. To all the world he looked like a healthy baby boy. But not long after my baby came, they took a sonogram and discovered that his heart wasn't closed. Dr. Boxer came into the room to assure me that he would be alright. "Don't worry, we can fix it," he said. "He'll be just like other kids, riding bikes and playing."

But I didn't believe him. His eyes told me a very different story. "Listen, Doctor Boxer, my mother was a midwife." I said. "I grew up around doctors and nurses. You're saying something to me with words, but your eyes tell a different story. This is not a good situation. I can see that. You do what you need to do to help him."

The four chambers of my son's heart were not divided the right way and his lungs were filling up with blood. They put a pace-maker in his chest to keep him alive in the hope that his chamber walls would close. The waiting was terrible.

We ran in and out of the hospital for nearly two weeks. It was tiring. On July the 2nd, Anthony's friends held a Fourth of July barbeque and we were invited. We decided to start the day at the hospital and then go over to the barbeque later and return to our son afterward. We thought it might be good to be with friends.

We tried to relax at the barbeque, which was difficult. We ate some of the food. I can remember sitting at the picnic table across from Anthony. His friend was beside me. I turned to that friend feeling a sudden rush of anxiety, "What time is it?" I said, and grabbed his wrist.

The watch read 9:30.

"It's nine-thirty!" I said.

"What is it Dorota?"

"We have to go Anthony!" I knew right then and there that something was wrong. Something was definitely wrong. I thought the worst and headed for the car. Anthony drove. On the way to the hospital, we stopped at the house to check the answering machine for any messages. In fact, there were ten messages. The doctors and nurses had called.

We had lost the baby at 9:30 PM on July 2nd.

A week before our baby passed away, I had had a second dream. This one was also vivid. The dream was of a full funeral at Holy Road Cemetery in Long Island. All the family was present. I saw a single bouquet of roses arranged in the shape of a heart, and everything lay under a torrential downpour. A rain so hard that people had trouble holding their umbrellas. A limo then pulled up to the cemetery, and the priest that married us stepped out and took out a little coffin behind him. The dream was so real that I was breathing heavily when I awoke. I told Anthony what I saw. And I told my mother as well. Neither of them could communicate with each other without me to act as interpreter, so they didn't tell each other about the dream.

When the day of the funeral came, everything happened exactly as I had dreamt it.

During the funeral, Anthony looked at me and said, "Don't ever dream again, Dorota." Then he walked away. We didn't speak of the dream again.

My mother said the same thing.

I often wondered what the black wedding dress could mean. After Anthony got cancer, I stopped wondering.

CHAPTER 4

FAMILY LIFE

W e waited a year before trying to have another child, and then I was pregnant. Soon after learning of the pregnancy, we found out that it was going to be a boy.

Maybe because I was one of two girls, I wanted to have a boy; more important to me, though, was to have a healthy child of either sex. In fact, I started to worry that he wouldn't be healthy, and that I would lose him as well. I was afraid. I had to know if he would be ok. I told the doctors, "You do all possible tests on me now to find out if there's anything wrong." Of course they ran all the tests they could run, some I'm sure they ran just to make me feel better.

The day I went into labor, Anthony came into the hospital room with me. The doctor asked him to hold me while they gave me an epidural. Well, that was more than Anthony could handle, and when the doctor took out that long needle to insert into my back, Anthony turned pale white and almost fainted; and yet I was the one having it done to me. The labor didn't turn out to be easy. It took nearly twelve hours to deliver Michael into the world. When he came, I was so worried he wouldn't be healthy that when the doctor showed him to me, all I could ask was, "Is he ok?"

"He's fine."

"But what about his heart?" I said. "Is anything wrong with him?"

"Mrs. Nigro, your son is perfect. There's not a thing wrong with him."

They were right, Michael was perfect and we were happy and so relieved. We were just beginning our family, and now the real work was about to begin.

In the winter after Michael was born, we were lucky enough to buy a house on Long Island in a town called Hicksville, about fifteen miles east of New Hyde Park and Anthony's boyhood home. We had been trying to put an addition on the old house in Williston Park for some time but the village, not to mention Anthony's brother, had made the process more difficult than we anticipated and had slowed our progress to the point where we had not even gotten out of the planning phase. Since we hadn't been able to expand the place we were in, we started looking for a way out of the house.

The trouble with that option was Anthony's older brother Joey didn't want to sell, and didn't want to buy us out. This meant that to a certain extent, we were stuck. But when our first baby died, Anthony's mother put pressure on Joey to let us out of the deal. I think she must have told him, "Either you let them buy the house or you buy them out. You take the house, they'll take the lot." It was a double lot, 100x100, so splitting it up was a real possibility. In the end, Joey and his wife decided to buy our stake in the home, and Joey went into his pension and gave Anthony $50,000. Anthony took the money and put a down payment on our new home in Hicksville.

We chose Hicksville for a lot of reasons. First of all, the taxes were about half what they were in Williston Park, so there was the financial aspect, but we also liked the community: the neighbor-hoods we looked at all seemed nice, not to mention we knew the town was in a good school district. After narrowing down the specific area, we chose our house because Anthony was adamant about buying a split level. He liked the separate entrance to the basement, which split levels have, because he wanted to use the basement as an accessory apartment, the income from which he intended to pay our taxes with, which he did. The house he found also had the added benefit of being within walking distance of the schools in town.

After moving in, we spent some time adjusting to our new life as homeowners and parents, but a lot of the adjusting revolved around our work schedules. A few years prior, the company I worked for, People Express, had been bought out by Continental Airlines, which meant we had to accept a significant pay decrease or quit. I chose to stay because I was still happy with the job. And while I worked for the airline and commuted to the Newark, NJ airport, which was still my base with Continental, Anthony contin-ued working as a diesel engine mechanic with the MTA. We both enjoyed our jobs. Commuting was always a pain, but when you're young and willing, everything is possible. I took longer, four-day trips, once a week, until we had children. At that point, I shifted my schedule and began taking day trips to Florida three times a week, which allowed me to be home more often for Michael. Our schedules were very flexible, especially mine, since I could choose the flights I worked around Anthony's schedule, which he chose on an annual basis. When the time came for Anthony to pick a schedule again, we talked about what the best fit for the family was.

Now, with the benefit of hindsight, there is one element of this period of our lives that I keenly recall, despite the fact that I paid little attention to it at the time. Anthony rarely brought his uni-forms home from the city, and he seldom wanted them washed at home. He had that done at work. Yet from time to time, for whatever reason, he would bring home a uniform. And I always knew when this happened because of the smell – you could smell the diesel fumes in his clothes. The smell, in addition to the fact that his new shirts never stayed blue, are two of the distinct memories I have of this time, which should have been red flags. Once he wore his shirts to the garage, the fumes, soot, and grease discolored the fabric so they never showed their original colors again. On the rare occasion that I did wash his uniforms at the house, they would leave a black grease ring around the washing machine drum. I remember running my finger across the drum and getting a black smudge on my fingertip. Knowing what I know now, I can just imagine what that environment was doing to Anthony's lungs, to all the MTA workers' lungs for that matter, if the fumes alone did that to his clothes. But we weren't thinking of those things then. We were focused on our family.

A year or so after Michael was born, I suffered a miscarriage, which was heartbreaking, but not as painful as the loss of our first son. Sweet Samantha came two years later. She was a designer baby. Well, that's what I say about her because I used the recipe to make her. You might say there's no such thing as a recipe to make a child, but I beg to differ; it worked for me.

I learned about the recipe at Michael's six-week checkup. His pediatrician told me a bit about himself. When he mentioned that he had both a boy and a girl, I asked, "How'd you manage to pull that off? Did you have some kind of secret?"

"Actually I did," he said. "I used the recipe."

"The recipe? What's that?"

"The recipe for a boy and a girl."

"Go ahead and tell me."

"If you ovulate on a regular 28-day cycle, have sex only four or five days before ovulation, and then refrain from it until two weeks later, you'll have a girl. Male producing sperm is faster than female, but not as strong, and so they get there quicker, but without the egg present they have nothing to fertilize and die out. Female producing sperm is slower and makes it to the egg just in time."

Well, I used the recipe and we got pregnant. After that, and despite my insistence that it would be a girl, Anthony was convinced it was going to be a boy. I think he felt this way because he was one of three boys and believed that he was destined to have only boys (on top of another reason that I would soon learn). He also didn't want to find out the sex of the baby at all after I got pregnant.

I promised him that I wouldn't find out as well, but when it came time to have the amniocentesis, which offered the first opportunity to determine the baby's sex, I couldn't help myself. Since Anthony had told me not to find out the baby's sex, and I had agreed, I felt like I couldn't ask directly. But that didn't prevent someone else from asking.

At that time, I had a babysitter for Michael who came to the house a few days a week when I couldn't be around. She went to the doctor's office with me that day, and when the doctor asked, "Do you want to know the baby's sex?" I motioned to her, "Why don't you tell Linda?"

He did. I could tell just by the way Linda's face lit up that we were going to have a girl. She had three boys of her own and wanted a girl herself and knew that I did too. Judging by her face it seemed she wanted to hug me. "Is it a girl?" I said – now I had to know for sure.

"Yes!" She said and hugged me.

When I found out, I couldn't believe it. "Now how am I going to tell Anthony?" I said, but that wouldn't take long to resolve.

When Anthony came home later that day he asked me how the visit went.

"Oh, the visit was fine."

"Fine! What do you mean it was fine?"

"Nothing." I said, but he knew right away what I had done.

"Don't tell me you found out?" It must have been written on my forehead.

"No, I swear I didn't"

He didn't miss a beat when I said that, "Yea, but you know."

At that point I had to tell him. Forgive me, but I made up a little story about how it happened: "When I went to sign my name," I said, "I saw the baby's sex written down on the paper. It was by mistake." I was very innocent.

He thought about that for a moment. He looked like he believed it. But he didn't seem like he wanted to concern himself with the "how" and the "why;" now that I knew, he wanted to know too.

"Well then, what is it?" he said.

"I'm not going to tell you, you have to wait."

"If you know, I better know. But it doesn't really matter because I know you're carrying a boy. You're carrying him the same way you carried Michael. It's a boy!"

"Ok, I'm having a boy," I said, "You're right, but you better stop painting that room blue and paint it pink instead."

When I said that he started crying. Then he called his mother and she started crying. I thought they were both crazy when I heard them, but that's when I found out that his mother's first child had been a girl and she had lost her. Anthony knew what happened to the first baby, his sister, and I guess the idea that there could have been a girl in the family always stuck with him.

Everybody on that side of the family was over the moon that Anthony and I were having a girl. Michael had two nephews, Mathew and Joshua, born to Anthony's younger brother Paul and his wife Sharon. Sharon, who was a "girly girl" (to the point that even her fur coat was pink), had given birth to two healthy boys, but she, too, had wanted to have a girl more than anything in the world.

So when we had Samantha it was like the heavens opened up; like the child could do no wrong.

"Oh, we're in trouble," I said to Anthony when she was born. "If we don't treat her like the other three boys then she's going to get it into her head that she's a princess." We stuck to that too, and more or less didn't let Samantha get special treatment.

As she was growing up, it became obvious that Samantha's personality took after Anthony's more than mine. She developed into a free spirit; a happy-go-lucky person who can relate to and interact with anyone. She's also very attractive: taller than I am and slim. When she walks into a room, eyes follow her, believe me, and I know because when I would pass by at that age no one looked at me. Well, not quite, but I certainly never got the same kind of response that Samantha gets. But that was still to come for her and for us, for the time being we had our young family to live inside of.

Anthony owned a boat, which he loved to spend time on. As the children grew, and we could all go out on it together, Anthony's favorite thing to do with us became boating. He had always owned one, but with a family on board, boating is a different experience than it is when you're a bachelor. Now we spent our summers on the South Shore of Long Island together. Zack's Bay off Jones Beach Island became like a playground, or we'd go fishing and clamming, or just hang out on the boat with the kids and their friends.

For the Fourth of July, we used to arrive in Zach's Bay early in the morning to watch the air show. The Blue Angels, or the Thunder Birds, were the highlight of the day. We lay on the bow and watched the jets fly over our heads, so low that you could feel the engines rumble as they flew off to Jones Beach. They were so close you felt you could just reach out and touch them. I will never forget my son's face when he saw the Blue Angels in Zach's Bay for the first time. His eyes and mouth opened wide. You could see they were like magic to him, and he couldn't stop talking about the jets for the rest of the weekend.

After boating, traveling became our second favorite activity and, since I worked as a flight attendant, traveling was very easy and inexpensive for us. The only thing we had to worry about was getting seats on the flight we had chosen. I can remember going to Boston for dinner at Faneuil Hall with all the kids in tow, or for a quick couple of days to Florida in the winter just to go to the beach. We tried to have fun whenever we could, and my flight benefits gave us a lot of freedom in this area.

We didn't just take quick trips here and there, but had as many international vacations as we could afford and fit into our schedule. Traveling with the kids was much more challenging than it was for Anthony and me when we were alone. However, we believed that travel was enormously educational, and given that our airfare was free, it was a lot more affordable than it would have been otherwise. Separately, we were aware that a number of people we knew had waited for their retirement to travel, at which point some had lost the opportunity. Confirmation of this fear came when our neighbor, Thomas Farrell, died. He and his wife, Catherine, had been waiting for retirement before they did the traveling they had always dreamed of doing. We took his premature death as a sign of what we already felt about waiting.

I can also remember that when we got married, we went to Australia and Singapore on our honeymoon. We spent two weeks overseas. It was wonderful. But when we returned Anthony's mother said, "You should concentrate on saving money and buying a house instead of traveling the world."

"You planned your life the way you wanted, I'll do mine." Anthony said, "I don't know what's going to happen, so if I don't make it until I'm 60, then I'm going to do it now."

What he said to his mother proved to be prophetic, but I never imagined that his death would come from cancer, I always worried instead that a bus would fall on him in the garage or he'd get disabled in some other way.

For these reasons, we travelled as much as we could, and chose destinations according to where we dreamed of going, rather than by what was easiest or most practical.

I remember once we went to Egypt and saw the pyramids. Anthony loved that trip. At home with Michael and Samantha, he used to watch National Geographic, and on one occasion they were showing the pyramids at Giza. "I'd like to go there," Anthony said. The kids agreed with him, and so I booked the trip. We flew into Cairo. This was before September 11, 2001, and before the new wars in the Middle East, so things seemed a bit safer. The kids were in middle school at the time, and when we returned, Michael was just so happy when the subject in his class was Egyptian history. It's one thing to learn about another place through the television, but it's more powerful to have been there and put your hands on the history yourself.

We started traveling more and more as the kids got older and it became easier. That's certainly one part of life I didn't need to regret when Anthony passed away.

Some of the bigger trips were to European countries such as Poland, Germany, Italy, France and so on. We went zip lining in Costa Rica, held koalas and watched kangaroos in Australia, and on our final trip as a family, we visited Lima, Peru. But of all the places we traveled, one of Anthony's favorite was my grandparents' farm back in Poland. Why he had such an attachment to the farm I can only guess at. He lived in New York and was born in Brooklyn, and he spent so many years commuting in and out of Manhattan, with all of its noise and stress, that I think the contrast to a quieter life on a European farm appealed to him.

He loved that village too. The first time we went there Michael had to have only been one-and-a-half or two years old, and Samantha hadn't been born yet.

I remember that when we entered the village for the first time, Anthony waived to a man and a woman on the side of the road.

They didn't wave back. This was just a small village where everybody knows everybody, and knows their grandparents as well, and we were driving through in a strange car with German license plates.

"Anthony, what are you doing?" I asked. "These people don't know who you are. That lady must be with her husband. And you're waiving at them."

"If I keep on waiving," he said, "One day they're going to wave back."

Don't you know, years later as Anthony and I started working to rehab the farm, those same people would come to the house and bring us fresh fish. The first time it happened, we were cleaning out one of the rooms and they came in and asked us if we were hungry. I guess waiving at strangers in a strange country can have a positive effect after all.

The first time we visited Poland, my father was still alive, so he had a chance to see Michael when he was small. At that time, the farm was running, but it wasn't in full swing anymore. My father was getting old, and yet he still planted potatoes, wheat and rye, as well as barley, but in much smaller quantities than my grandfather, and he still had a couple of chickens running around.

Anthony was blown away by the simple facts of life on the farm. A big revelation for him was that we made our own butter. My mother and father had reconciled by this point and lived together on my grandparents' farm, and for that trip anyway, they were together, although still divorced.

At the dinner table during our first visit there together, sitting among the numerous meat and vegetable dishes was a loaf of bread that my mother had baked in her brick oven that afternoon. The bread tasted delicious, but Anthony focused on the butter she had put out with the bread. I guess he was surprised by the taste because he said, "Is this real?" When he asked me that, I turned to my mother and translated what he had said. She looked somewhat perplexed, and then she smiled.

"Yes, she made it a couple days ago." I said to Anthony.

"What do you mean, she made it?"

"She makes it, Anthony." My mother began talking then, and I explained what she was doing, "And she's making more now." At that, my mother went back to the kitchen and came out with a wooden barrel with a wood lid and a stick inside. Then she showed him how to churn the butter as she filled the barrel with cream. True to form, he sat there holding that thing and beating and beating until he'd made butter.

"Oh my God," he said when he finished.

My mother scraped the butter off the side of the barrel. He looked at the butter then as if it were the product of a nuclear reaction when it was done. They had made about four pounds' worth, and it was as yellow and as fresh as can be. We never went shopping for food when we were on the farm, we never needed to, and who wanted to when the food all tasted so good.

Now, Anthony loved going there. The simple things in life make you the happiest.

But why wouldn't he have enjoyed himself on my grandparent's farm? He was generally given the royal treatment by my family, and by everyone in town who knew us. On top of the treatment he got from my family, my friend Barbara also cooked and baked everything that Anthony liked whenever he came to Poland. So that was two houses we could go to where he was treated like a king. We used to go to Barbara's house and she and her mother would turn dinner into a giant production. Her mother didn't speak any English but she wanted to talk to Anthony throughout the dinner, and so I would have to translate back and forth as everybody at the table started talking. At times, I'd get confused and start speaking in Polish to Anthony and in English to Barbara and her mother, and then everyone would laugh. They'd actually get a little pushy for me to translate faster so they could keep the conversation going.

When Anthony began eating Barbara's mother said, "Barbara, make sure he has potatoes and vegetables." She was so concerned that he was given the right treatment.

That's when I started to notice how men were treated in that country. Not long after her mother asked to have more food on Anthony's plate, Anthony saw that I needed some vegetables. He motioned to me, then he picked some up in a serving spoon and put them on my plate. Barbara's mother was practically in shock that he was serving me and not the other way around. When I saw Barbara's mother watching us with interest, I started giving her a bit of a hard time by asking Anthony for more helpings of food from the large serving bowls around the table, which he dolloped onto my plate without hesitation. I think Anthony saw what was going on because he played it up a bit. Men serving women, even innocently, was not done here, and I had never realized it until that moment that Poland was so oriented toward serving men.

I started to think back to my childhood years in Poland. Serving men went so far that my mother used to get everything ready for my father's bath, and when he came out she had it all laid out by the sink for him. She used to stick her hand into the bathroom and give him his shirts and pants. Well, the times were certainly changing, and Anthony and I represented that change.

We went back and forth several times to Poland, and on each occasion, Anthony seemed to enjoy himself more and more as he became more comfortable and familiar with the people and the places.

When my father died in 2004, I flew back to Poland immediately to complete the arrangements for his funeral. I wanted to bury him with his parents, but by the time I got there one of my cousins had already arranged to have him buried in a different part of the cemetery.

I heard about what she had done and spoke up, "No, that's not happening."

My cousin responded, "The arrangements have already been made." When she said that I pointed to my hand and said, "Blood is thicker than water. I'll make the arrangements my father wanted to have." At that, I went straight to the funeral home and undid the plans my cousin had made to implement the ones my father had wanted, "I want my father buried with his parents."

The people at the funeral home took care of it. The section of the cemetery he requested happened to be full, but we were allowed to bury him there because his own father had been buried there back in 1973.

Later, I was present with Anthony when the workers opened up my grandparents' crypt to place my father inside. That was a unique experience. "I can't believe I'm watching this," I said to Anthony. He didn't hear me though, he was leaning over the opening, curious to see what was inside.

"Oh, it's my grandfather's skeleton," I said, and when I did, his skull shifted a little. It was very strange to look into that crypt and to see him exactly as he had been positioned some thirty years prior; his suit wasn't even destroyed. It looked the same as the day they put him in there. It was made of gabardine nylon; I guess that lasts forever.

With little or no ceremony, they moved his bones and consolidated them together in a separate box and then put my father in the space they made inside.

My mother died a year later in 2005. When she did, Barbara made all the arrangements for me. All I had to do was pick up the casket and pay for the priest's taxi. The priest, who, by the way, had his own new Mercedes parked out in front of the rectory, still needed me to pay for the taxi.

My mother always complained about my father, and she left him and went back to him on more than one occasion, but she always loved him. When she died, I found a copy of my father's picture stashed inside her address book. I would have buried her right next to him, but she had told me that she didn't want to be buried with his family, and so I found a separate location for her final resting place.

Now with both parents dead, the farm passed to my sister and me. My first thought was to go ahead and sell it, but Anthony wouldn't hear of it. He dreamed of spending his summers there, away from the fast lifestyle, and fixing the place up. And it was beautiful; the farms surrounded by woods and fields where you could take walks and, along the way, pick mushrooms and berries. Winter would have been a little tricky since at that time they didn't plow the streets of the village – maybe a plow would run through once in a blue moon.

But Anthony loved the idea. He wanted to raise pigs and chickens. He was even enamored of the outhouse on the property of all things. On one occasion, we arrived from New York to find that contractors had torn it down. They took it to the back somewhere. Well, Anthony went and found that old outhouse and put it back up. "Why are they taking my outhouse?"

I didn't bother answering that question, "Whatever makes you happy," I said.

We really were getting the farm ready to live on. We had the floors all refinished, and the rooms repainted, and the kitchen redone. He saw it as a place to retire to, and we spent a lot of time flying back and forth. We had the trip down to a science.

I'd work the flight over to Germany, and he'd fly along with me, only he would be seated in first class. There he'd eat a salad and some bread and then sleep the whole flight; again, who married whom for the benefits? Once we got to Poland we would take the crew bus together to the hotel where I changed and showered, while he got the rental car. From there, which was Berlin, Germany, we'd drive over to Świebodzin, Poland and the farm. He was fresh from sleeping the whole flight over, and I'd try to catch a wink or two in the car, but he always made it difficult because he drove so fast on those little roads that it would keep me up, or I would wake up in the middle of a multi-car pass he was undertaking. I'd hear the engine racing, and look up. His driving nearly made me afraid to sleep while he was behind the wheel. I feared I'd open my eyes and we'd be in a ditch on the side of the road or wrapped around a tree, or that I wouldn't open my eyes at all.

We were blessed to have been able to live this way for so many years. As the kids got older we did spend more time at home, punctuated by trips to Poland to work on the place, but their formal education became more of our focus.

While academics came easily to Michael, and consequently he always did well in school, Samantha was a different story all together. Education was never her central focus. She even failed math her sophomore year of high school in 2008. In this instance, she had to take math again during the summer and attended school five days a week for six weeks, while we had to postpone all our summer plans. Anthony got as upset as he could with Samantha that summer, after all, he was her protector. "I'm going to make your summer miserable." He said. I don't know if he actually tried to make her summer miserable, but the fact that she had to go to school five days a week on her summer vacation probably did that on its own. After that, the importance of school sunk in for her a little more than it had before as she realized that her GPA would play a major role in deciding where she would end up after high school.

Two years after Samantha had summer school, Anthony began to indicate he wanted to retire. He was getting tired of commuting into the city every day for work and all that entailed. Traffic on Long Island was getting worse. I delayed this day some when he first began bringing the subject up to me, but I couldn't delay it forever. I knew he was working on the farm with an eye to retirement. I told him, "Anthony, what are you going to do at home by yourself? I don't plan on joining you. We have two kids in college. We need money. Our pensions are not going to do it." And while he listened to this argument at first, it wouldn't be long before his drive to retire cancelled out any argument I could make against it.

CHAPTER 5

RETIREMENT

Despite my opinion on his retirement, Anthony had made up his mind to go through with it. I still wasn't thrilled with the idea, but I knew that wasn't going to stop him. He planned to work on the house, and if he needed to make himself busy, or if we needed the money, he said he'd get a job driving a school bus, which he had obtained a license to drive when he was at the MTA. "There's always something to do if you're willing to work," he said.

I knew he was serious, but I only found out exactly how serious when he called me up one day out of the blue to ask about which pension plan he should select.

"I'm here at the benefits department in Brooklyn," he said. "What should I do?"

"What do you mean?"

"Well, I have a choice of three plans."

Of the three pension plans he described, the highest benefit, and first choice, was based on his final salary, but if he died, it died with him. I wouldn't get a thing. The second choice offered the death benefit but was five-hundred dollars less per month. The third benefit he didn't bother describing because I cut him off.

"Come on, honey," I said, "We have two kids in college. You have a pension, I have a pension, we have Social Security, and we'll have property to sell. And look at you, you're as strong as a bull, I'll go before you. We have children in college, and we need money; five-hundred dollars is a big difference – go for it."

I wonder how many MTA employees over the years made the very same decision, only to have their spouses die in six months or a year, leaving them with no further pension income whatsoever. When you work for a union or for a large company for a number of years, the retirement package and benefits plan is part of the reason you complete the time there. In hindsight, having an option that offers more money up front but cancels any death benefit seems immoral when you realize that MTA workers, and specifically those occupying certain positions in the MTA, such as mechanics, die much younger than either the national or the state average. The question itself forces retiring workers onto the casino floor when they retire. The problem is, people don't work to retirement age for 20, 30 or even 40 years to take a gamble at the end. Why offer to drop the death benefit as part of the package at all? Why put workers in front of a slot machine as they go out the door, gambling that they'll live to see the full payout they sign up for?

At my suggestion, Anthony picked the highest pension and declined the death benefit. He completed all the paperwork that day, supposedly correctly, at the benefits department of the MTA. He was leaving that company after 28 years of service, but he was ready for a change.

He started the retirement process in March and was officially retired on August 29th of 2011. But around the time that he began initiating his retirement, he started coughing. The cough persisted. I thought it was just a cold, and I yelled at him as he left the house in freezing weather wearing a jacket over a t-shirt. He didn't even bother to button it up.

"What's wrong with you? You have a cold, and you can't even bother to button your coat. You're going to make that cough even worse."

We never thought anything serious was wrong, it just seemed like a cough. He went to the doctor to get it checked out and they gave him medicine. After that, it almost went away.

Soon after his course of medicine ended, his cough returned. It had never really ceased, and in mid-May, it came back full-blown and seemed to be getting worse. By June, around the time of my daughter's graduation from high school, it got more persistent still. It was at that time that we were getting ready for Samantha's graduation party. In preparation, Anthony wanted to improve the backyard by expanding the pond and by turning the little brook we had into a waterfall. He wanted my help because I was better at envisioning the final product. He was the muscle, I was the brains, so to speak. In order to decide on the final height of the falls, we agreed to keep on stacking cinder blocks until we reached an elevation that fit with the backyard landscape, which was difficult to see on paper. We went up about three blocks, at which point we thought it was just right for our pond and stopped, then we began adding rocks to finish it off.

Anthony stood inside the pond wearing a pair of waders, while I handed him the rocks from outside on the grass. To me the rocks felt heavy, but for him they shouldn't have been, and yet I noticed that he struggled as he lifted each one of them. He must have felt it too, because it wasn't long before he said, "You know what? I'm losing my strength. I don't know what's wrong with me." All the while he was coughing.

Something was wrong with Anthony, but at that point it wasn't clear what it was, and we were busy moving forward.

Sam had a beautiful high school graduation party at our house. All told, we had about 75 people in the backyard. Anthony held court, as usual, talking and laughing with his cousins and everyone else, but he coughed right through the party even though he had gone back to the doctor and gotten more medicine.

Afterward, he knew he had to find out what the heck was wrong with him, because it wasn't getting any better. The medicine was just a Band-Aid.

Soon after the graduation party, he went to an ear nose and throat specialist in the hope of finding the source of his cough and maybe even a cure. On top of the cough, or really, I guess what induced it, was what he called a tickle in his throat.

The doctor examined him and said, "You should go to a gastro-enterologist because I have a feeling you have acid reflux, which is causing that tickle."

Anthony agreed and we went to see Dr. Santa Nandi where he had an endoscopy. It was August 28th; he officially retired the next day. We knew Dr. Nandi because I had previously gone to her for tests and felt comfortable with her. But everything turned out fine in her examination of Anthony. The one piece of advice that she gave us was to come back for a follow-up, which we planned on doing.

In the meantime, and now that Anthony was retired, I put him on a diet.

I used to make him a healthy lunch every day when he worked for the MTA, but he never lost any weight. I also know that he never lost any weight because he liked to have a buttered roll five times a week at work, and whatever else he would buy when he was there. Now that he was retired, he wasn't going to eat like that anymore, as far as I could help it.

I told him why I was doing it, too, "Every day I got up in the morning and made you a salad and chicken, but you never lost any weight. Now that you're home, I can control what you eat."

He rolled his eyes, but he also knew that he had been unhealthy in the past, and with his cough lingering, he wanted to make an effort to eat a little healthier, and possibly extend and improve his life.

In that period before his follow-up with Dr. Nandi, I noticed that Anthony was getting tired and weaker. Something wasn't right. His cough just continued getting worse and worse, as bad as it already was. He was also losing weight. I saw that his love handles were disappearing, which I took as a sign that our diet was working.

"You know, I noticed my pants don't fit me anymore?" he said. He was wearing his old pants which were a size 34. He hadn't been that thin since I met him.

During that summer, he spent a lot of time out on Zach's Bay, fishing and clamming and just being out there. He was also planning to fix up a Model T Ford that he had owned since he was a young man. Anthony always imagined that he and Michael would restore the car together. Most of the guys at work knew what he was planning to do since he had bought the old car with his father a long time before in New Jersey, back when his parents owned a house on Lake Hopatcong where they spent their summers. Anthony's mother and grandmother used to spend the entire summer in the lake house, while Anthony's father worked all week and drove in for the weekend. This was before they moved out of Brooklyn and bought the house on Long Island in New Hyde Park.

Anthony and his brothers were out with their father at the lake one day and saw the car and bought it as a project to restore as a family. I guess it never came to fruition. After their childhood, they held onto the car, first storing it with Anthony's brother Joey. Years later, after we had gotten married, Anthony bought his brother out of the car and then stored it in our one-car garage in Hicksville. Of course, storing a defunct old car got more difficult as the kids began driving their own vehicles and parking them in our driveway.

The problem Anthony encountered was that finding free time to work on the Model T was difficult. He did buy a few items for it here and there, and had the house full of parts catalogues, which I still have. I think he even brought the catalogues to work, because many of his coworkers knew about the old automobile and his planned restoration. Working on that car would have become his focus in retirement.

At the end of summer, we traveled to Poland to work on the farm house. Neither of us knew that this trip would be our last together. But I wonder if maybe Anthony did know, down deep somewhere, because as we left, he lingered when he said, "Goodbye" to Barbara. In fact, he grabbed her and gave her a long hug and kiss.

She was surprised by how emotional he was in parting. "Why are you hugging me and kissing me like this, you're acting like you'll never see me again?" she said.

"Well, you never know," he said.

His behavior in that moment remains with me until today. Maybe there were certain things he didn't say or do at that time just to protect me.

We returned to Dr. Nandi for the follow-up appointment in September. When she saw Anthony she said, "Anthony, you lost quite a bit of weight." As I already mentioned, his love handles had disappeared, but when Dr. Nandi mentioned it, I realized that he was looking thin and gaunt.

"You'd lose weight too if you had a little gestapo at home watching every bite you took: salad, chicken; chicken, salad; fish, salad; salad, fish, again and again and again. God forbid I have a piece of New York cheese cake every once in a while."

Dr. Nandi smiled, but as Anthony continued to joke he began coughing. Dr. Nandi then turned away from him. I saw her face as she did so. She was in shock. She looked like she saw a ghost. Anthony didn't notice her reaction.

She seemed to reflect on what she heard in his cough, and as we were leaving, she called him back and said, "I don't like your cough, and I don't like the loss of weight." She scheduled him for a chest x-ray, as well as abdominal and pelvis sonograms. She asked that he get those done immediately.

We had all the tests done the next morning. Anthony's x-ray didn't show anything, but when he was having his upper sonogram done, the technician was going up and down on his chest with the probe. As she did that I saw him wince. "That hurts," he said. And with that reaction, she ordered him back to get a CT scan.

They sent the results on to Dr. Nandi the next day. I got the call from her on the morning of October the first. Anthony was sitting beside me in our home. She said, "Dorota, I don't have good news to give you. You and your husband need to make an appointment with an oncologist immediately. Anthony has Stage IV lung cancer and it doesn't look good." While I was reeling from what she had told me, she went on to say words that terrified me more than the diagnosis, "Dorota, please don't fly to India so much. Stay with your husband."

I understood what she was trying to tell me, and Anthony saw by my face that something was wrong.

"What's the matter," he said, "What did she say?"

I just looked at him.

"You have Stage IV lung cancer."

CHAPTER 6

CANCER

We sat in complete shock. Tears streamed down my face. I couldn't speak for several minutes. Dr. Nandi had given me a phone number for an oncologist in Woodbury, and I eventually roused myself from my grief and called to make an appointment. I had to do something. We had to do something. However, that appointment wasn't set until October the 28th.

It was difficult to get my footing in the light of his cancer because his condition deteriorated so rapidly. Anthony got visibly worse nearly overnight after his diagnosis. His cough became more and more consistent. He was soon coughing up blood. On the 7th of October I took him to the North Shore Hospital in Plainview where we were given an appointment to consult a pulmonologist by the name of Dr. Peter Weil. After reviewing Anthony's CT scans, Dr. Weil referred us for a bronchoscopy. Anthony was then admitted into the hospital on the 10th, and the following day had the procedure conducted by Dr. Lawrence Scherman, who viewed Anthony's airway in detail. His scope came back "inconclusive." We then met for a follow-up appointment with Dr. Weil who scheduled Anthony for a second bronchoscopy to be performed by Dr. David Zeltsman in early November.

In the meantime, I was falling apart. I visited our family doctor, Dr. Yelena Stone, for help on October 15th. I knew I needed something to get me through. The pressure I felt to help guide Anthony's treatment where I could, and support our kids, and keep the house from falling to pieces, combined with knowing that I was losing my husband, was getting to be more than I could take.

"You need to put me on something," I said in her office. She knew about Anthony, so she understood what I meant.

"When I get up, if I sleep, my mind's racing; my heart's racing. I don't know if I've slept or if I haven't. I need something to function, but I don't want too much. I still need to drive. I don't want to be sleepwalking."

She gave me Xanax, "Take only 0.25 milligrams a day," she said.

I listened to her advice and thanked her for the prescription, but that wasn't all I had come for that day. "I'd like to speak to somebody who can tell me straight what our options are with Anthony. I feel like they're sugar coating too much."

I felt as though there was something more, something else I needed to find out.

"The only doctor I would recommend to you is Doctor Kessler," she said. "He'll tell you the truth. I've known him since college. If I had cancer, he would be the one I would go to."

She gave me his information, and as soon as I got home, I called him. I took the first appointment they had, although that wouldn't be until December.

I couldn't worry much about the timing of that distant appointment because Anthony was having difficulty at that very moment. I was angry at the idea that his first bronchoscopy had come back inconclusive. Cleary, something was wrong with his lungs and throat. He couldn't stop coughing.

I couldn't wait until November for the second bronchoscopy. Without telling Anthony where we were going, I packed him up and took him to the emergency room at Long Island Jewish Hospital in Lake Success, where he had been scheduled for the procedure with Dr. Zeltsman.

When I got on the Long Island Expressway, Anthony said, "Where are were going?"

"I'm taking you to the hospital for your bronchoscopy."

"The emergency room. I can't wait in there."

"Don't worry, Anthony. You won't have to wait."

I dropped him off in the waiting area of the emergency room and went up to the window. "Look, my husband has cancer, and he's been coughing up blood today. I found him on the floor of the den with blood on his chest and neck. This can't go on, something has to be done." I was lying, but I had learned to lie if Anthony was going to get the treatment he needed and in a timely manner.

Dr. Zeltsman conducted the second bronchoscopy the following day, and found Anthony was in such bad shape that an operation to remove the cancer was impossible. This finding makes me believe that what Dr. Scherman discovered in the first bronchoscopy looked so bad that he wanted a second opinion.

In the short, but terrible, span of time from his diagnosis, Anthony summoned up a courage that's difficult for me to understand. He had gone, in a matter of hours, from a relatively young man with decades ahead of him, looking forward to an early, and well-funded, retirement, still with children to guide and grandchildren to meet, to someone whose remaining time was measureable in months. He handled his fate with grace and without self-pity. He didn't go to pieces no matter how bleak his situation or inane and infuriating our experiences with the American health care system.

We endured a period of emergency room visits and appointments that alone left us feeling ragged. All the while, I witnessed too much time wasted on what appeared to be a system of care centered around paperwork, systemic procedures, limited patient interaction, avoidance of liability, and the endless pursuit of money, often at the expense of everything else.

I recall the Polish health care system was less complicated and ridiculous under the Communists than what we found on Long Island. My mother worked in the medical field for most of her life. My uncle was also a doctor. Patients in a hospital did tend to wait a good deal, though that happens here as well, but in the Polish system I encountered there were no consultations or referrals. We didn't pay for visits; there were no copays, or paying for the procedures out of pocket, and so there wasn't a constant pressure to discover who (or what entity) was going to pay for which procedure and how much they would or could pay. While we had other difficulties to overcome in Poland's socialist health care system, we at least never felt as though the patient was being efficiently bled of every last cent before their bodies turned cold. On the other hand, in Poland, doctors' salaries were low. I recall that I made more as a teacher in the United States in 1983 than my uncle made, and he ran the hospital in Poznan, Poland. Little money, and a monolithic control structure meant there was little or no competition between doctors, or even competition to improve local or regional hospitals, and so few of the doctors seemed to take an interest in patients. Only seldom, however, did I make comparisons between the two systems because I was busy doing the best I could to save my husband.

As the weeks passed, and Anthony's cancer aggressively grew, we encountered more difficulties in getting straight answers. I felt the nurses and doctors were minimizing the gravity of the facts and presenting us with a slate of options for coming procedures without advising us on what to do in the limited time it seemed obvious we now had. Of course, we knew what Stage IV lung cancer meant, but we needed to hear the truth, every step of the way. I wanted a clear-headed, fact-based portrayal of our options, and yet that kind of advice proved difficult to come by.

Was chemotherapy really necessary at this point? Was it going to be beneficial compared to what it would take from him? It's difficult enough to make these decisions under pressure when you feel you're being passed off to the next paying procedure.

A few days after his second bronchoscopy, we headed to the appointment we had made when we first learned he had cancer. It was now October the 28th, 2011; however, our visit wasn't as informative as we'd hoped. When we met, Dr. Irina Murakhovskaya viewed all of the x-rays and sonograms from Dr. Nandi, and specifically asked Anthony what he did for a living.

Anthony explained his job, including the fact that he worked with diesel engines. She listened, and then scheduled him for chemotherapy. She was compassionate and seemed informed, but what she didn't do was connect Anthony's job at the MTA to cancer, or even mention that such a possibility could exist at all. But how could she not know? Why wouldn't learning that he had been a diesel mechanic for over 28 years with the MTA raise a red flag in her mind? There certainly had been others from the MTA who passed through that same oncology center with similar diagnoses.

Having since learned a bit about the connection between breathing diesel fumes and cancer, I look back on our experiences with some confusion. While the WHO, for instance, didn't state, unequivocally, that breathing diesel fumes absolutely contributed to both lung and bladder cancer until June of 2012, the World Health Organization's International Agency for Research on Cancer had publicly classified diesel exhaust as "probably carcinogenic to humans" in 1988 – 23 years prior to our 2011 doctor appointments.

I've never been able figure out if the doctors we consulted, particularly the oncologists, whose professional lives were focused on cancer, somehow didn't know about the diesel-fume-cancer link, despite the public nature of WHO statements, or if they knew of the connection, but for some reason didn't tell us.

Had I known of it earlier, I don't know what I could have done in the short time-frame, but knowing would have been a big benefit to us emotionally. Anthony and I were desperate for any degree of clarity on anything related to his cancer. We felt blindsided by his diagnosis, and helpless in the face of our confusion about it, and we had no context in which to understand what was happening.

It would, unfortunately, take until December, and our meeting with Dr. Kessler, for us to finally learn of the environmental connection between Anthony's job and his cancer. But by that point, Anthony had less than a month to live.

In the face of Anthony's worsening condition and the intransigent health care bureaucracy, and in lieu of meeting Dr. Kessler in December, I spent hours on the computer looking for answers and for help. I spoke to doctors from various cancer hospitals. I searched, "best thoracic surgeons in America" on the internet and came up with one Dr. Richard Feins in North Carolina. Dr. Feins was recognized by his peers as the best thoracic surgeon in America in 2011. I decided to contact him. To my surprise, he not only responded, but agreed to view Anthony's medical records and then speak with me on the phone. He called me just days after our first contact, and spent quite a bit of time discussing Anthony's medical situation with me. Most of what he said was a reiteration of what we'd been told before by various doctors, including Dr. Zeltsman, who had performed Anthony's second bronchoscopy.

Dr. Feins further reiterated Dr. Zeltsman's position that Anthony couldn't survive surgery. "If I were to touch him," he said, "I think it would surely kill him." Anthony's lung cancer was so advanced and widespread by that point that his body couldn't handle the trauma of surgery to remove the cancer, and the extent of the cancer's spread was too great to even try.

Dr. Feins was polite. "I'd be happy to treat your husband," he said, "But you have excellent doctors on Long Island, and Dr. Zeltsman is among the best."

Maybe it has to do with my personality, or maybe it had to do with the fact that I felt as though Anthony and I had been getting the runaround now for a month, but when Dr. Feins told me that Dr. Zeltsman was among the best, I tested him. "How do you know Dr. Zeltsman?" I asked.

"I met him once at a conference," he said. I would have pressed him further but he went on to describe the man to me in detail. Maybe he sensed where I was going. After that I felt confident that he was at least telling me the truth, and I accepted his diagnosis and stopped looking outside of Long Island for treatment.

Anthony, however, didn't want to undergo the chemotherapy.

I begged him, "How can I live with the fact that I didn't do everything for you."

"Honey," he said, "They're not able to do anything for me, and you can't either."

Despite his objection, and the toll he knew it would take on him, he consented to undergo the treatments.

Anthony was in and out of the hospital now every couple of weeks. His cough continued to worsen and they put him on oxygen.

Anthony was hospitalized again on the 4th of November at North Shore Hospital in Plainview. That stay happened to coincide with the date he had been scheduled to have chemotherapy – the first in the series on the 7th, 8th, and 9th - at Woodbury. Because Anthony was, at the time, an inpatient at Plainview, it was logical for him to receive whatever medical treatment he needed there.

The oncologists in Woodbury, however, complained some about his having the treatment administered in Plainview. When they did so, it began to dawn on me that their interest in my husband might not be entirely centered on his health. My suspicion about their motivation would turn to certainty in the very near future.

Anthony stayed in the hospital for several days after the chemotherapy ended. I felt like I was going to pieces, and found myself having trouble sleeping. I started searching the internet again frantically and late into the night wondering if by some chance, we could do something more for him that we weren't already trying; or that I might find a treatment or a bit of information that could help. Of course, medical miracles happen, but with Anthony the prognosis was bleak. I couldn't come to grips with the idea that I was going to lose him – that we were all going to lose him – and so suddenly! How could he go so fast?

During that time, Anthony's cough, as bad as it had been, worsened. Michael, Samantha and I visited him as often as possible whenever he was in the hospital. Sam was there every day after school. Michael, on the other hand, had a hard time visiting his father and seeing him in that state. The decline was so rapid and his appearance so shocking that it was difficult for everyone to take, but Michael took it the hardest.

Every time he went to visit, he felt weak and close to fainting. When Anthony had a procedure to drain the fluid and seal part of his lungs in the second week of November, and just after his chemotherapy, I insisted that Michael come to the hospital to see his father. He came right after school, after the procedure ended. While in the recovery room, Michael suddenly reached out and grabbed the curtain for support and began looking this way and that for a chair to sit in. We had to catch him before he fainted.

Not only was my husband dying before us, but the toll it was taking on my children was becoming harder to bear.

While Michael didn't spend much time in the hospital, he did talk with his father often on the phone which kept them in contact. I was grateful for this, because Michael and Anthony had always been close. It was agonizing, however, to watch as Anthony's illness progressed and brought with it the increasing nearness of the end of their relationship.

During this period too, Anthony had a lot of visitors in the hospital and at home. Neighbors, friends, and especially cowork-ers came to see him on a regular, if not daily, basis. When they saw him, their faces typically reflected disbelief. The suddenness and extent of his decline was difficult to understand, and at that point we didn't have any idea what had caused his cancer.

Johnny Nowakowski, who was a childhood friend of Anthony's, stood by my husband's side almost every day. They had boated and fished together right up until the time of Anthony's diagnosis. He was in the hospital nearly as much as I, and used to bring Anthony whatever he needed.

My girlfriend Mary was also there whenever I had to leave for work. She had learned of Anthony's cancer right after we did, and in an almost equally cruel manner. We went out to her cottage in the Hamptons to help repair the water damage it had sustained during Hurricane Irene. "You lost some weight?" she said when she saw him. "Are you on a diet?"

"I stopped eating bagels."

"You lost that much weight by not eating bagels? You sure ev-erything's all right? Maybe you should see a doctor."

"I have." He said. "I've got Stage IV lung cancer. Now can we get to work." With that he walked into the house and started tear-ing down drywall. Mary looked at me. "We just found out about it." I said. "He doesn't want to stay home."

I flew only once a month for work at this point, and Mary used to take the day off from her own job to keep Anthony company on those occasions and whenever else I couldn't be there. Both Mary and Johnny Nowakowski showed us what good friends are; in good times and in bad.

As much as I appreciated the help we got from our friends, I was surprised and saddened by the lack of response from Anthony's family. Anthony's parents were older and couldn't handle seeing their son in that condition. But I expected at least a call from someone on that side, especially since every passing day seemed to give us another scare, and another battle to fight. In other words, we needed all the help we could get.

Since Anthony was hospitalized so frequently, and North Shore Hospital in Plainview was only miles from our house, and he was comfortable at that hospital, I asked to have his next round of chemo scheduled there instead of in Woodbury.

Plainview had a small, comfortable room with just four or five chairs to accommodate that number of patients, and a good view from the windows, beyond hospital grounds. The window was high enough that you couldn't see the parking lot below and you sat ten feet or so away from the window, which offered a view of the sky and the trees; unlike the Woodbury room which was very large and provided no view whatsoever. You just looked at the other patients around you, and at the equipment and the sterile decor. It was like mass production for human treatment, and very depressing.

At Plainview, Anthony had also developed a good relationship with the chemo nurse, Corrine Wyllins. They had similar personalities. She was strong and passionate. He opened up to her. When I met with her after his first, three-day round, I asked her about Anthony because I knew he hadn't been opening up to me, but I got the impression that he might have opened up with her. I was curious.

"Did he ever cry?" I asked.

"Yes, he did," she said.

He never cried in front of me or showed his emotions, and I was relieved by the fact that he was comfortable enough there and with her to cry if he needed to. I knew he kept a strong face for me. I appreciated that as well.

In that same conversation, I asked Corrine if I could book Anthony there for the final set of chemo. He had already been there for the first round, and was both comfortable at that location and with Corrine. It obviously made sense to complete the series there.

"Sure, I can schedule it for you," she said, and put Anthony's name down to receive his final chemo series on the 7th, 8th and 9th of December, 2011.

Later that week, having just learned that Anthony would not be returning to their facility for his last treatment, the doctor in Woodbury called us.

His call taught me something. The only time we ever got a fast response from them was when we canceled expensive procedures. The doctor didn't seem very happy that we had taken the chemo elsewhere, and he also didn't want to take "no" for an answer regarding this last treatment.

"I'd like to schedule your husband for chemo." He said.

"My husband would like it in Plainview."

When I said that to him, he responded, "We can't put him there, they only have four chairs."

"But my husband wants it where he had the others. He's comfortable there."

"We can't put him there because it's all booked," he said. "It only has four chairs."

We went back and forth for a moment until I said, "Dr. Kappel, my husband will have it in Plainview."

"It's booked."

"I know it's booked because I booked it. My husband will get what he wants. And you have to sign off whether you like it or not. And if you don't sign off, we won't get it at all, because it doesn't matter anyway."

We were talking about twenty-thousand dollars per day for chemo. When they first saw my husband at Woodbury, they had booked both three-day sessions at once, which amounted to one-hundred-and-twenty-thousand dollars. Now, they didn't want to let go of this last piece of the pie.

I was getting to know how, if not outright corrupt, then convoluted and wasteful American health care really is. Health care now reminded me a lot of my husband's job with the MTA, or Poland under the Soviets, but worse, and for the profit of hideous monopolies and conglomerates. The process always seemed designed to maximize profits for the hospitals and doctors.

The procedures themselves are difficult enough to endure, but waiting for them, and the mental fatigue of navigating the crooked system, is nearly as bad as suffering the illness.

CHAPTER 7
NOT JUST A NUMBER

We left Anthony's last chemo series at the hospital in Plainview in silence and drove to Dr. Leonard Kessler's offices in Rockville Center. I had hoped that he could give us a straight answer about Anthony's condition, but there wasn't much hope at that point. For Anthony, heading to another office after chemo must have felt like a marathon.

As we approached the intersection of Old Country Road and Jerusalem Avenue, Anthony perked up and asked a strange question that temporarily took my mind off our visit with Dr. Kessler.

"Are you going to get remarried after I'm gone?" he asked.

I had been waiting to meet Dr. Kessler for four weeks, just to maybe hear that my husband wasn't certainly going to die, so remarriage was about the farthest thing from my mind at that point.

"Are you serious?" I said. "How can you even ask me?"

"Honey, we've had a beautiful twenty-five years together. If I could change the outcome, I would. I'd love to have another five or ten years with you guys, but I can't, and you're still a young woman and have so much to offer. You deserve to have another twenty-five years with someone else."

My mouth dropped. "Is there something wrong with your head, Anthony? You just finished your chemo. I'm on Xanax, and your mind's on me getting married."

"You deserve to be happy," he persisted.

"Look, we don't have to go to Dr. Kessler's if you don't want," I responded. "We can go home. I'll cancel the appointment. He's not going to tell us anything we don't already know, anyway."

"I know you better than that, Dorota," he said. "You need the doctor to confirm what we already know, or you won't stop thinking about it, so let's go and get it over with."

With that, he leaned his head back, and I continued driving.

After meeting the receptionist, we waited inside Dr. Kessler's office for a few minutes before he walked in with Anthony's file in hand. He had barely introduced himself when he looked at me and said, "You, go and get yourself a good lawyer."

"Why do I need a lawyer?"

"Mrs. Nigro, what your husband has is environmental."

"Environmental?" I echoed.

I couldn't understand what he meant by that. How could it have been environmental? Anthony didn't bat an eye, however, "Don't you see, Dorota?" he said to me, "It's diesel!"

I wanted to ask Dr. Kessler more questions, but Anthony wasn't interested in learning more about the effects of diesel fumes - he was living them. Instead, he asked the doctor the one question he had been waiting to ask for weeks: "How long do I have to live?"

"You're lucky if you make it to spring."

On the way home, Anthony and I drove in silence for a while. Anthony sat looking out the window, then suddenly he turned, and said, "I'm ready."

I hadn't known what to say since we got into the car, but his words set me off. "Ready! Ready! Do you think this is all about you now?"

He tried to respond, but I continued, "Christmas is coming. The kids are taking finals and finishing the semester, and I'm not ready for you to go now."

He focused on me then, like he couldn't believe what he was hearing.

I continued, "I need people's names, phone numbers, names of garages you worked at, job descriptions. Then you can go, but not now; not until after Christmas."

At first, he looked a little baffled at my outburst; then he realized that I was planning to fight his company.

He said, "Oh my God! Dorota, are you going to fight my company? Are you really that thick? You can't! You'll never win! They have a legal department. They have lawyers coming out of the woodwork. You're going to get sick over this. It's not worth it. I'm just a number. Don't you get it? I'm just a number to them!"

It pissed me off when he said that. "I'm already sick!" I said. "I'm losing you. If it's the last thing I do I'm going to get your company. You're not a number to me and you won't be a number to them when I'm finished. You might not be able to see me do it, but I can promise you, it will be done."

We drove the rest of the way without saying another word. I was furious. Anthony watched me as I drove, wincing in pain here and there from the unevenness of the road.

When we arrived at the house, I helped him walk up the stairs and into the house. We walked in silence. But all the while I couldn't stop thinking, "They killed him! They killed him!"

In a moment, it all came back to me: the smell on his clothes, the black soot that stained everything, even the walls of the depots and nearby buildings and his shirts and the washing machine. It was diesel. Diesel fumes were the reason he attended so many wakes.

Many times, over the years, I had found Anthony taking his suit with him as he got ready to leave the house in the morning.

"What's that for?" I'd say.

He'd tell me that someone had died and he was attending the viewing, but it happened so frequently that I almost had trouble believing that was what he was doing.

"Listen, Anthony, I might be Polish but I'm not stupid, if there's someone else in the city then go, please, just go."

He'd laugh at that, but I was serious; sadly, so was he. He really was attending all those wakes for MTA employees, and they died so frequently because the fumes they were exposed to were killing them.

How can you spend 40 hours a week breathing air full of carcinogen and not get cancer? The answer is that you can't. But how could it be? Why didn't the workers fight? Why wasn't it publicly acknowledged that diesel fumes in MTA garages were giving their employees cancer? Was it not considered important enough to be newsworthy? This was Manhattan after all, not West Virginia. New York City, so I had always heard, is the greatest city in the world; how could this happen here?

I didn't have much time to dwell on what I had learned, as Anthony needed to be hospitalized the next day. I felt crazy at that point. I started to think that Anthony might die then and there, and that I had to get answers from him, answers that would help me to fight back and give him a voice. Preparing to fight his company also gave me a sense of direction in the face of his impending and needless death. It was the one thing we could do that would have an effect.

I started calling lawyers to the hospital whose names I found on the internet, and began asking Anthony questions from his bedside and taking notes. I needed details about his job and about his company. I made a list of depots and dates when he worked at them, as well as his job descriptions, and the names of people he knew and their phone numbers.

The lawyers I called started showing up at the hospital, but after they talked with us nobody would take the case. How could this be? I thought. He's dying. They did this to him. Maybe they were the wrong lawyers. I got the impression they thought they couldn't win. I had called one lady who came all the way from Pennsylvania to see us, but she also declined to take the case. She did, however give me a piece of advice. We rode down in the elevator together and she said to me, "Can I suggest something?"

"I can't," I said. I had a feeling where she was going. The conversation with her and with the other lawyers had pointed in this direction.

"Be a smart woman, do a partial autopsy. Call the pathology department."

The next day I called them and they told me how it would be done. I never told Anthony about it, and I was never sure if I would go through with it when the time came, but I would face that decision down the line.

The next ten days in the hospital were difficult. Anthony's breathing was more strained. He had fluid removed from his lungs to make his breathing easier. He also refused to eat. I cooked his favorite dishes and brought them to the hospital, but he still wouldn't eat; in addition, he was slowly reducing his fluid intake.

"Why are you not eating?" I asked him.

"It's self-destruction." he said.

I shook my head. "No!" I couldn't face the idea of life without him, and I couldn't bear the thought of him doing anything that would further shorten his time.

Michael called his father nearly every day, but he still couldn't handle seeing Anthony like that. Samantha spent most of the evenings with Anthony after school. I don't know what they said to each other then, but I know it had a dramatic effect on her. Both children proved very strong in this terrible time. And it *was* a terrible time too, one that blurred the days together like a painful nightmare.

On December the 20th, I arrived in Anthony's hospital room to find the infectious disease doctor there. He frequently checked on Anthony at this time. I could tell by their demeanor he was discussing something important with Anthony. The doctor greeted me with a smile and said, "We have to make a decision about moving Anthony to rehab."

"Rehab?" I replied. "You mean hospice? No. Absolutely no."

In response the doctor said, "Dorota, you don't know what you're up against."

"What I know is that he is my husband. I might be only 5'2" but I am much stronger then you are. Tell me what I need to do and I can take care of my husband. I want him home for the holidays."

The doctor had no choice but to agree, and I went home to prepare the house for his return. I put the Christmas decorations up first. It needed to at least look like Christmas. Then I worked on making the sunroom comfortable for Anthony to sleep in. It was his favorite place in the entire house, and also much easier for him to access than our bedroom.

Anthony came home the next morning. He also returned with a million pills from the doctors for me to give to him.

The pills made me further question the treatments: why did he have to take seven different pills four times a day? Just to sell the drugs? On top of that, I knew that many medications were cheaper in India. As an example, in India, and without insurance, a Z-Pak sold for a buck. While the same five-day dosage sold for thirty-nine dollars in the United States. I know this because on one occasion Michael got sick on the very day we had an insurance coverage lapse, and I had to pay the outrageously inflated price out of pocket.

Anthony heard me complaining.

"Just give me the painkiller," he said, "Don't worry about the rest, they can't fix this."

Christmas came in short order.

I invited Anthony's parents to spend Christmas Eve with us. I made fish, as always, and we had a nice quiet night. Anthony's family spent Christmas Day at his younger brother's house. His parents were supposed to stop by on the way home, but they didn't. On the 26th, some of his family and friends came over to keep us company and to enjoy the holiday as much as possible together. Many people come to visit with us then, including friends from Florida, and Anthony's best friend Johnny as well as others. Anthony was happy to see everybody. He knew that he might not see them again.

Those nights, I slept in the recliner next to Anthony. He spent most of his time in the hospital bed in the sun room. I don't think he slept at all because I caught him watching me on a few occasions. At one point in the night, Anthony asked me to lay down next to him.

"I'm afraid I'll hurt you."

"Dorota, I'm almost gone."

After that he started hallucinating.

"What are those three people doing here?" I looked up when he said that, startled that someone might actually have been in the room.

"Those three Peruvians at the door?"

"Peruvians? Oh, honey you're hallucinating."

"Oh yeah, you're probably right."

"Why did you think they were Peruvians?" I asked.

"I don't know."

On December the 31st we decided to watch the ball drop in Times Square on TV as we always had, but we fell asleep before we saw it. We awoke the morning of January the 1st next to each other. There was something different about Anthony that morning. I sensed that he wanted to talk. He told me how much he loved me. He said, again, that he wished he could spend more time with us, but that it wouldn't happen.

I said, "Anthony, I will always love you. How can I handle things without you? I don't even know how to pay the bills online." He just smiled and said, "Dorota, you're the strongest woman I ever met. You can handle anything that comes your way. Let's go, I'll show you how to make payments online." I helped him downstairs to the computer in the den, where he signed into our bank account and proceeded to explain to me the entire process of online banking.

When we went back upstairs to the sunroom, he turned to me and said, "It's time."

"Not today. We have too many memories New Year's Day, give me one more day." I said.

On January the 2ⁿᵈ, in the afternoon, Anthony asked me to call the fire department to take him back to the hospital. I did as he asked. The Hicksville Fire Department arrived not long after I placed the call. An ambulance and a few fire trucks came with sirens and lights on. About six men walked into the house to take Anthony to the hospital, including our neighbor, Justin. Justin's father, Thomas Farrell, had died of a heart attack thirteen years prior; he had also been my husband's friend as well as his boss at the MTA.

The men showed Anthony great respect when they took him out of the house. Their presence and demeanor made his departure touching, almost ceremonial.

After putting Anthony into the ambulance, and having a word or two with him, they drove him back to Plainview Hospital nearby, where he would stay.

January the 4ᵗʰ came, and Anthony asked me to help him to take a shower in the early afternoon. I did as he asked, and helped him to get to the bathroom and under the water. There he apologized to me, "And that's what I didn't want my wife to do for me."

"What? Wash you?" I responded.

"Yeah, or you should have done it sometime before I got sick," he smiled.

"Anthony, you're still thinking about it?" I asked.

"Of course. I'll stop thinking about sex when I'm dead."

In the evening, Michael and Samantha came to say goodbye to their father. I was there as well.

I returned to him the next morning. I didn't think he was going to die that night; I just didn't feel that it was going to happen. When I arrived, he was sitting in bed waiting for me. I entered the room, and he asked me to pull the curtain shut, which I did. I then sat on the chair next to his bed. We held hands as we kissed. We each said, "I love you," and "goodbye," and then he asked me to leave.

"Why?" I said.

"I have to go. I can't go when you're here."

"That's just too bad," I said. "I won't leave."

"Then I can't go," he said.

"Then we'll sit here until hell freezes."

He just shook his head at that, gave me one more kiss and pointed to the door. "I love you."

I got up and left the room. Tears started pouring down my face. For the first time, I couldn't control myself. I passed the nurses' station where Anthony's doctor and one of the nurses were standing. I heard the nurse say to the doctor, "She's leaving." I assumed they expected me to stay with him to the end, and I looked up and said, "He doesn't want me to be here now." I continued walking to my car.

I was home in fifteen minutes, and as I walked in the door I heard the phone ring. When I picked it up, the doctor said, "Mrs. Nigro, we lost Anthony. He left us at 10:53 AM."

"I'll be there."

As I put the phone down, I felt pain in my chest. I could hardly breath. Samantha and Michael were in the house. I hadn't said a word to them yet, but they overheard my conversation with the doctor. It was very difficult to see them when they knew their father was gone. We just held each other and cried. I didn't know what to say to make it easier for them to deal with his death.

After a time, I can't say how long, I called my husband's friend Larry to let him know the sad news. He offered to make all the arrangements and I accepted. I also called Anthony's younger brother, so he could let his parents know.

After that I went to the hospital by myself. I entered his room, and saw him there lying motionless. He looked as if he were sleeping. I kissed him one more time as a final goodbye, and just before I left I whispered in his ear, "I'll make sure you're remembered. You're not just a number. I will always love you."

On the way out of the hospital, I stopped at the admission office and requested a partial autopsy.

CHAPTER 8

OUR CHILDREN'S STRENGTH

The hardest part is seeing your kids in pain.
Before I left to return to the hospital, I saw my son cry for the first time. Samantha was a mess.

Once the three of us were calmer, I called my husband's friend Larry. He went to the funeral home to make arrangements for us. It was the same funeral home that had handled his wife's passing. I also called my neighbors. When I left for the hospital they came to help. Anthony had passed before 11:00 that morning. Our neighbors arrived by 11:30.

Something odd stands out in my memory though: when I went back to the hospital, I didn't drive myself. My girlfriend Fran's sister, Adrianne, from New Jersey drove me. I don't even know how or when she got to my house from New Jersey, or why she would have been there in the first place. I just remember her asking, "Dorota, do you want me to take you back to the hospital."

"Yes," I said.

She made that difficult trip much easier. I was without Anthony now, and the shock of it was setting in, but at least I wasn't alone.

In the hospital I said "Goodbye" to Anthony, and then in the office I had some difficulty when I asked for the partial autopsy. The nurse looked at me like there was something wrong because ordering an autopsy when the cause of death is known is not normally done. "You can call Dr. Kaplan if you want," I said, "but I won't let my husband leave the hospital until I know a partial autopsy is going to be done." They agreed and took him to Long Island Jewish in Lake Success where they performed it. I went back home.

When I arrived, I found food waiting. Our neighbors had gone to Costco and picked up a tray of sandwiches. They also got a tray of shrimp because they knew Samantha was vegetarian. We have a very close neighborhood, and thank God they were there to help us.

Soon Larry arrived to drive me to the Robert White Funeral Home so I could finalize a few things. There were questions he couldn't answer without me. I had to pick out the coffin that would be displayed during his funeral, and tell the funeral director that Anthony asked for a cremation.

I also set up the viewing for Sunday, and explained that we were going to have a closed coffin.

Samantha protested that decision later on, but I wouldn't budge from it. "Absolutely not," I said, "Your father didn't want me to see him when he died, and I don't want you to see him in a casket." He wouldn't have appeared the way she remembered him at all. And I didn't want that image on her mind. I think it would have stayed with her.

I'm happy we went with the closed casket.

Sunday came, and we got prepared for the viewings. The first was in the afternoon, and was to be followed by a second later in the evening.

Death affects different people in different ways. Some people take it better than others.

That Sunday morning, Samantha was in her room getting ready, and Michael had gone to the store to a get a few things.

I was still preparing for the day when Anthony's older brother Joey and his mother came by with the sandwiches. My father-in-law, who had just gotten out of the hospital, stayed at home. They were kind, and I was happy to have the sandwiches, even though I didn't have much of an appetite and wasn't eating any of it. My mother in law was 88 at that time, and she was taking it very hard.

She sat at the dining room table and Joey sat in the sunroom, eating the food they had brought. I went back to getting ready.

When my mother in law noticed that I wasn't eating she said very kindly, "Why don't you eat something."

"I'm not hungry."

"I know, but have a bite or two."

"Ok," I said, and I took a few bites of the sandwich.

At that point Joey came out of the sunroom.

I said to his mother. "At least he's not suffering anymore." Joey was passing nearby me at that moment. When he heard what I said he responded, "Yeah, maybe he'd still be here if you'd taken him to the right doctors."

"Excuse me?" I said. I was practically in shock that he would have said such a thing. "How is it possible that I could have taken him to the wrong doctors?" I said, getting angrier. "Where were you and your girlfriend the nurse in the last month of your brother's life? We hardly saw you. Your brother was in and out of the hospital for three months. You were there a couple times. . ." I trailed off.

I still had more to say to him, and I was getting ready to say it too; believe me, I was just warming up, but at that moment Samantha stormed into the room from her bedroom. She must have heard what Joey said. She was hardly eighteen at the time, and while she was no pushover, I never expected to hear from her mouth what she was about to say. She stood beside me, pointed her finger at her uncle across the kitchen counter and said, "How dare you come to my father's house and disrespect my mother. Get the f**k out of my father's house."

His eyes got huge when she said that. My mother-in-law, who already looked traumatized from the moment she entered the house that morning, appeared even further stunned by my daughter's words.

"Do I make myself understood? You are not welcome in this house anymore. Get out of my father's house."

He did as she said and she followed him and opened the door for him and screamed behind him, "and don't bother coming to my father's viewing at all."

When he had gone, she turned to me and said, "When I get married, I don't want to see his name on the invite list."

I didn't know what to say. I almost felt as though my husband were speaking through her, because he would have responded similarly.

Outside, as Joey left, Michael was just walking up the front walkway, without any idea what had just happened. As he passed Joey, his uncle said, "Your mother has issues," and continued walking.

Michael didn't know what he was talking about. He said, "Whatever," and came into the house.

I wasn't as upset as I might have been after the ordeal, as the gravity of the circumstances far outweighed any one person's childishness. In addition, Michael, Samantha and I needed to focus on finishing our preparation for the viewing. I don't know when my mother-in-law left my house.

When my children and I arrived at the funeral home, we saw both that it was packed, and that in spite of the crowd, people continued to stream in. I never expected such a crowd. Seeing it lifted my spirits some. So many people came in and out that it was hard to keep track. But I remember Mary reading the eulogy, which was very good. She read as a slide show ran behind her on the screen. The kids had told her to make the eulogy happy, and to try to make people smile rather than cry, and so that's what she did. She told several stories about Anthony, or Tony, as she and his friends called him.

One of these stories sticks out in my mind:

There was a guy at Anthony's job who bragged he could drink any kind of liquor without ill effect. When Anthony heard him brag about his prowess he piped up and said, "Oh yeah, I bet you can't drink Polish Spirytus," which is Polish straight grain alcohol. The guy responded that he could drink it, so Tony brought a bottle into work. There wasn't much left in the bottle, but enough for him to get the point. Anthony handed the Spirytus over and the guy drank a glass, while Anthony stood there waiting for him to start gasping and choking, but nothing happened. "Isn't it burning?" Anthony asked him after a few seconds with no reaction.

"No, it tastes like water."

"What?" Anthony said and grabbed the bottle. He smelled it, then tasted it. "Son of a Bitch," he said. "I'm gonna kill those kids." Of course, neither of the children would admit to having done it. But after the funeral someone went up to Mary and told her that it was Michael and his friends who drank the Spirytus.

People smiled as Mary told her stories. Music played in the background as well, and I think the music was playing on one of the kids' iPods, because in the midst of Mary's eulogy, the song "Don't Worry, Be Happy," came on over the speakers. People laughed then. Anthony always used to sing that song, and say those lines. The moment gave everyone in the room a touch of happiness in the sadness, and a reminder of Anthony's personality.

The kids asked Mary to read her eulogy again for the evening viewing, which she did. A lot of friends and neighbors showed up for that viewing, and Michael and Samantha were happy to hear it read again.

Many of Anthony's friends and coworkers, and even some of the union representatives handed me their business cards that day.

They told me that if I ever needed anything, I should give them a call and they would help me. These were promises I hoped to be able to rely on in the near future. I kept their cards because I knew that sooner or later I would need them. I also think this is how I later got connected with one of my husband's friends, a man who was making an issue out of the poor ventilation at the MTA and the cancer the workers suffered. But I was in no shape to fight then, or to even remember everything people told me that day.

We held the funeral at Holy Family Church. Three buses full of Anthony's coworkers came to show their support for the family and mourn their friend and fellow worker.

When I entered the church, I was immediately struck by how full it was. Anthony's mother and brothers had already arrived when Michael, Samantha, and I walked in (Anthony's father was not well enough to attend). The coffin sat in front of the altar, and as we approached, I could distinguish a cross on top of it. The three of us filed into the first row and waited for the funeral service to begin.

During the funeral mass, at the point at which you turn around and shake people's hands, Samantha's uncle, Paul, leaned toward her and gave her a kiss on the cheek. He said something to his brother then too about shaking hands with Samantha, but Joey declined to do so, and also told Paul what he thought of Samantha, which she also heard.

I, on the other hand, barely knew what was going on around me in the pews. I kept my hand over my mouth as the priest spoke. Tears poured down my face in silence, although every time I looked around the church I felt strengthened by the fact that so many MTA employees attended his viewing, and now the funeral.

I thought again about all the viewings Anthony used to attend, and my confusion over the years regarding how and why so many MTA workers seemed to die shortly after, or even before, they reached retirement. How could so many people die? Now they came to his funeral, and I understood what many of the men and women who worked for the MTA already knew: the job killed them. And the frequency with which they died had helped to organize them into a constant funeral procession. The group of coworkers who attended the funeral even used MTA buses to get there. I still don't know how that was arranged.

The MTA's huge presence at Anthony's funeral and viewing left one question in my mind: if the job was killing them at this rate, why had no one done anything about it?

The following days were very empty for me; they still are in some respects. Anthony's friends kept in touch to see how I was doing. Some of them even lifted my spirits by telling me what Anthony had said about me and our family. I never heard from either of his brothers or my sister-in-law, Sharon. Yet Anthony's friend from work, James Dockerty, not only visited Anthony in the hospital on numerous occasions, but kept texting me and telling me how strong I was; he told me that at work, Anthony used to comment about my strength. He further told me how proud Anthony was of his son and his daughter; how he talked about our travels around the world, and our trips to Poland and the farm. Anthony knew how to live his life, and he enjoyed every day as if it were his last.

Just before Anthony passed, he told me that he had lived a happy life. If he had to do it all over again, he would live it the same way; he had no regrets.

I returned to work a week later. It was difficult to get back on a plane and work in front of people, but I managed. Work also helped me to heal in some ways.

I resumed my Newark to Delhi and Mumbai routes, picking up extra trips to augment our reduced income. My friends at work were my main support. While I go back 30 years with many of the people there, I think the most therapeutic part of working again, if you can call it therapeutic, came from the fact that I seldom flew with the same group of flight attendants. We changed our schedules frequently, which meant that nearly every time I stepped on the plane in those early weeks, I spent the better part of a day locked in with a new crew, which was surprisingly helpful. Constantly talking about my husband's death and repeating the story over again let me air out my feelings, so to speak, and made it easier to get over the terrible situation. After a while there were no tears left, or almost none anyways. I had described it so many times that it wasn't as raw of a wound as it had been earlier on.

At that time also, another of my husband's friends made a huge difference in my life. I didn't know who he was at first. But he started speaking to me at the funeral and afterward. Anthony's death had made a huge impact on him and motivated him even more.

The MTA had employed him as a ventilation specialist. He held that job for thirty-five years, which meant he knew a lot about the way things in this area functioned at the MTA. After my husband's passing, he created Anthony Nigro's Committee which was a platform to help raise awareness about the effects of diesel fume inhalation. He also began speaking at numerous diesel conventions on the impact of diesel fumes on human health, bus depot ventilation and the MTA's negligence with regard to maintaining and updating their air handling equipment.

In the future, he would invite me to come to those diesel conventions, but in the immediate aftermath of Anthony's death I wasn't focused on digging into the evidence surrounding what caused it. For the time being I still needed to heal, and with what had happened with Joey on the day of the viewing there was plenty of healing still to do. His behavior, and his childish words had caused a clear rift in the family that involved my children.

I knew we couldn't sit at a table with Joey so we stopped spending holidays with the family. I didn't give up on Anthony's parents, however. I continued to call and check on them. I wanted the kids to have a relationship with them as much as they could.

Michael's grandfather adored him. I think it's in part because Michael is a great deal like my husband Anthony. He loved to listen to his grandfather's World War II stories, and Michael is a good listener just like Anthony was. Prior to Anthony's death, we often saw the family altogether once a year at the family picnic in the summer in Eisenhower Park. Anthony loved to barbeque; he would set up tables at 5 o'clock in the morning to make sure everything was just perfect for everybody. You had to go really early to get those benches or else you had to bring your own.

In time, my son Michael would take over my husband's role at the family barbeque. He barbequed and talked with and met everyone. The way he acted made it almost like it was before, which was bittersweet, but still sweet.

What Samantha had said to Joey however would linger on. Before every holiday, her grandmother would ask me to prompt Sam to apologize to her uncle. On one particular day that I happened to be off from work, her grandmother again suggested that Sam apologize for what she had said to Joey. "You have to tell your daughter," she said. But I had heard enough. I didn't think that Sam had anything to apologize for, and I asked my mother-in-law if I could come over.

When I arrived we sat and had coffee, then I said, "My daughter is your granddaughter. She's the only one you have and the only one you'll ever have. She is your blood. I can walk away from the family, but you can't walk away from those two kids. If you have an issue with my daughter, here is her phone number. I did my job, I raised her right. You, on the other hand, are protecting a 60-year-old man with no control over his mouth. You want my daughter to apologize, you call her and ask her yourself.

"Your granddaughter is just like your son Anthony, very strong. So you call her and tell her to apologize to your son, but I warn you, you will lose your granddaughter if you do that."

I never heard anyone mention that Sam had to apologize again.

CHAPTER 9

TROLLEY GARAGE

A month after Anthony's funeral, a friend of his from the MTA introduced me to an attorney named John Dearie. At that time, Dearie was two years into a major civil lawsuit against General Motors on behalf of transit workers. I was the 125th person to join the suit, which was nearing completion and seemed reasonably likely to win. Dearie clearly thought so, or he wouldn't have invested so much of his own time, energy, and money in it.

I didn't know how I was going to fight back, but I had to start somewhere, and this lawsuit gave me a way to begin.

At the same time, I also found myself fighting the MTA for my husband's post-retirement death benefit, something I didn't even know existed when Anthony first passed away. Fortunately, one of his friends alerted me to it.

Apparently, there had been a retiree who had made the same choice that we had to forego any death benefit. This person died in a motorcycle accident shortly after his retirement date, leaving behind a financially devastated family. This motivated the Transportation Workers Union, Local's 100 and 106, to begin lobbying the MTA to allow beneficiaries of workers who died within three years of their retirement to collect benefits.

Two years after that process began, in May of 2012, the MTA agreed to allow a death benefit under certain circumstances.

I was entitled to this benefit because Anthony had passed away within months of retiring. Had he died outside of that window, due to the benefits package we had chosen, any and all compensation to us would have ended with Anthony's death.

The decision to choose a retirement option with no death benefit had seemed so simple when I had believed that Anthony would outlive me; now I question the forthrightness of the entire process and its design. Simply put, what appeared to us to be a reasonable gamble on the odds of Anthony living a number of years beyond his retirement, was, for anyone informed of the MTA's data, a poor bet.

Obviously, any time an employee contributed more to the MTA's pension fund than he drew in retirement, the difference accrued to the pension fund. Given that the MTA knew the frequency with which mechanics died, the pension fund's no-death-benefit pay-out option was one the MTA knew was weighted in its own favor.

As shocking as I found this, it was not, unfortunately, my sole conflict with the MTA over benefits. In addition to the obstacles built into the process of pursuing the benefit, it turned out that, according to the MTA, neither I, nor my children, were officially listed as beneficiaries. While Anthony had originally named his father as his beneficiary, later, when he and I got married, he changed it to me and then added the kids. From then on, and for nearly a quarter of a century, we received statements in my name, and later in the children's names as well. But now, as I attempted to collect the benefit I had only just learned I was entitled to, I was informed that I was not, in fact, the beneficiary at all. We were told that when Anthony had initially updated his beneficiary after our marriage, he had failed to appropriately initial a correction he had made on the form. He had, in fact, inadvertently begun writing his father's name on the change form. He then crossed that out and wrote my name. Now the company was interpreting this to mean that the beneficiary had never changed from the original beneficiary, my father-in-law.

I called the MTA to correct the obvious error, but they didn't see any need to change it. I thought I had a better chance of solving the problem in person and so, on my day off, I went to the MTA offices in Brooklyn to dispute their silly decision. Inside the office, I found three people working in a huge room full of empty cubicles. With so few people, and no line, I imagined that I might get somewhere.

I was wrong.

I asked to speak with the person in charge, but the lady who spoke with me wouldn't let me talk to the manager directly. Instead, she insisted on walking back and forth between the cubicle where I sat and the cubicle where the boss sat to relay messages between us.

Protocol, I suppose.

I would have found it comical had I been there to address a less crucial issue. But after she had made two or three trips between her manager and me, I realized the process was designed to ensure that any attempt to accomplish anything would be an exercise in futility.

To make matters worse, assuming that I could correct the named beneficiary, it was unclear if and when the MTA would get around to actually dispersing those benefits.

The MTA was retroactively working its way through the list of entitled beneficiaries starting with their oldest cases, which meant they might not even reach the most recent deaths for years.

Standing in that office in Brooklyn made me feel as though I were back in Poland again, under that awful, grinding, and inhuman system. I had, however, learned one thing from the Polish and their terrible, Soviet-style bureaucracy that would serve me well in this instance: You never accomplish anything unless you know somebody.

In this instance, my husband's former job partner, Steve Czubay, who checked in on me from time to time after Anthony's death, proved invaluable. He told me where the Local 100's offices were located in Manhattan, and informed me of a union meeting taking place a few weeks later. He thought that attending the meeting might provide my best opportunity to directly approach a union representative to sort out the mess. The only problem with this plan was that I wasn't invited. Steve didn't think this would be a problem. "Just go there," he said, "I think you can get in."

I took his advice, and when the date came I dressed in my flight attendant's uniform and went over to the building where it was being held. It might seem funny that I dressed in a uniform, but trust me when I tell you that people treat you differently when you're wearing one than when you're not. I wasn't above using whatever I had at my disposal to get my way.

I entered the building. A man stopped me in the lobby. "What's your name?"

"I'm Anthony Nigro's wife," I said.

He called upstairs, and after a moment or so the call came back that I could go in. Upstairs, I walked into a meeting of about 100 people. Many of Anthony's friends recognized me. Three of the union representatives met me and took me to a side office, where I showed them my paperwork pertaining to the death benefit. I understood that having the beneficiary changed was going to be a tall order, but I hoped that they might at least have the ability to expedite the payouts.

"Here's a copy of the policy you passed entitling the beneficiaries of an MTA retiree to collect death benefits if the retiree dies within three years of retiring. It's something for which I'm very grateful. However, it appears that your benefits department lacks the staff required to implement it properly. My husband was a union member in good standing for three decades, and I don't want to wait until I'm 80 to get what you owe us."

They agreed to help, and within a few weeks, my father-in-law received his son's death benefit in a onetime payment, which he then dispersed to my children and me.

We were happy to have the money. I've heard of spouses losing their houses and more when their husbands died after retiring and the money on which they thought they could depend never came. I felt lucky to receive even a penny of it.

While fighting the MTA for the death benefit, I began learning all I could about diesel fumes and their consequences. I began attending forums in Manhattan and Brooklyn on the dangers of diesel fumes and the particulates it carried. These forums often consisted of scientists, chemists, doctors, and lawyers making speeches or discussing their findings in large auditoriums. Speakers from all over the world attended.

This was at a time, in 2012, just before the WHO (World Health Organization) pronounced that diesel fumes were carcinogenic, and so a lot of information that had previously garnered little attention was making its way to the public.

I attended every forum held in New York City. One conference I attended, which was generally representative of the others, occurred around a year after the WHO's statement about the relationship between diesel fumes and cancer. This was the New York/New Jersey Education and Research Center's 34th Annual Scientific Meeting – Diesel, Transportation, Occupational Exposures, and Health. It was held on April 5th, 2013, at the Mount Sinai School of Medicine in Manhattan. The conference focused on the need for clinicians to "understand the link between diesel exposure and health, as well as the need to develop new technologies to reduce diesel exhaust." I learned a lot. There was so much to know, and there was so much information about the negative effects of diesel that it was hard for me to get my head around all of it, or to understand why it had taken so long for the pronouncement.

To see all these scientists and lawyers show their findings on what diesel fumes did to humans, and the occupations in which workers were most vulnerable, was both enlightening and enraging.

Not only had almost nothing substantive been done about the dangers of diesel fumes for 70-plus years, but no one had won a lawsuit in any court or workers compensation board linking diesel fumes with lung cancer.[*]

And yet the MTA itself had begun adding major air filtration systems to its buildings beginning in the late 80s and early 90s. Obviously, running buses inside a garage is not good for air quality, but how could a city have gone so long without making an effort to improve conditions for their workers? It's not as if men were not getting sick and developing coughs and dying in the 1950s and 60s, they were.

When my husband started working, health care was part of the package at the MTA, and had been for a long time. This means that even before the 2012 WHO statement that confirmed the supposition of the organization's 1989 statement announcing the probability of a link between diesel fumes and cancer, the MTA's own records must have reflected that their employees, on average, died at an age significantly younger than those in almost all other professions.

Compiling data on life expectancy in an effort to project insurance risk (the work of an actuary) has been done for hundreds of years. It's inconceivable that the MTA failed to employ this risk assessment tool. In other words, the company had to have known.

One union representative sent me data from a ten-year study for the Local 100, which was my husband's Local. The study was conducted by NYCERS (New York City Employees Retirement

---

[*] "On October 1, 1990, diesel engine exhaust was declared to be a carcinogen subject to Proposition 65. On October 1, 1991, the warning requirements under Proposition 65 became effective for diesel engine exhaust. See Health and Safety Code § 25249.10(b)" from: https://www.envirolaw.org/documents/Buses1stAmendedComplaint.pdf

System) and covered the period from the year 2000 to 2010. During that time, 6,500 members retired at an average age of 59; in that period 8.5% of those retirees died. The average age at death was 62 years old. Local 100's website states that the union represents 41,000 workers, mostly in New York City transportation. Considering that life expectancy for New Yorkers is about 80 years, those of transit workers is, by comparison, short. Specifically, the average life expectancy for New Yorkers as a group is more than 29% longer than the average life expectancy of MTA employees as a group based upon numbers in this study.

Because the union's study was based on the aggregate age of all MTA retirees who died within that ten-year period, however, rather than on data for only those working in proximity to running buses, the results don't reflect the degree of early death for people like my husband. The gap the study showed would inarguably be much bigger if the MTA data was confined to bus mechanics who worked the morning service. There's no question that the mechanics, and those with other jobs in proximity to the running buses, died, on average, earlier than those whose work didn't require them to spend their days breathing in high volumes of diesel particles.

Ultimately, this means that for MTA bus mechanics, the gap in life expectancy between them and the average New Yorker is likely far larger than 29%.

There are more comprehensive numbers still. What company pays for workers' health care and insurance and doesn't keep these kinds of statistics? I've talked to people who have seen the numbers. Unfortunately, I haven't been able to get my hands on a copy. Winning the release of those numbers, as far back as they are available, would provide precise data detailing the dramatically shorter life expectancies of MTA mechanics compared to those of its other employees, and to those of the general population.

The longevity rates of MTA employees are the historical record of workers in New York City. Such numbers should not be hidden from the public eye by either corporate prerogative or law, or destroyed. It does no good to keep the numbers secret.

If I learned anything from living under the Soviet Union and behind the Iron Curtain, it's that the truth will always come out, justice will have its day.

It seems certain that the MTA had to have known what was happening to its employees by the late 1980s, at the absolute latest, when the WHO declared that diesel was "probably carcinogenic."

How could the fact that diesel fumes were giving their workers cancer not have been an openly known secret by upper-management? As I mentioned above, the death of MTA workers at or around the time of their retirements was so well known it had become a stereotype.

When my husband began working for the MTA at the Walnut Street Garage in the Bronx in 1985, the conditions were almost the same as they had been thirty or more years prior. In fact, the city was, in many places, still using buildings converted from other uses to house and maintain their diesel bus fleets, and the worst garages to work in were those that had been converted. Such garages had not been designed to house idling diesel buses. Two of the old trolley garages still online when Anthony began working were the 100th and 54th Street garages. The conditions inside those garages were terrible. The garage at Hudson Piers had been a loading dock before it was converted for diesel bus use, and the Walnut Street location had originally been built as a warehouse. The conditions in these "barns" was appalling, as not only had the garages not been designed to house idling diesel buses, but the MTA itself had done little or nothing to improve the indoor air quality or to reduce bus emissions since gaining full control of the mass transit system in 1962.

The MTA didn't focus on better air quality in earnest until sometime after my husband began working there. When they did, they began phasing out the old infrastructure for new, purpose-built bus garages and depots, and installing catalytic converters on the buses themselves. I've also been told by the men who worked with Anthony that in the early 80s, in many locations, you couldn't see from one side of a garage to the other for all the smoke.

One retired bus driver, who chooses to stay anonymous because he fears reprisals, told me that he remembered, "shifting at the old 100st depot, [where] there would be a blue haze in the depot without any ventilation except some open windows . . ."

Another of Anthony's friends and co-workers, Paul Santiago, who's a retired bus mechanic, explained:

> I worked with Tony for years in the old KB [Kingsbridge] depot and the Old West Farms depot and Walnut depot . . . I worked midnights so by default I was working when all the busses were fired up in the morning. I remember one morning working in the old Kingsbridge depot sitting in the Twin Doughnuts [store] across the street seeing for the first time the amount of black smoke that was spewing out of the door I [had] just walked out of that led to the basement level. Above the door was a huge black streak on the wall all the way to the roof.

In Addition, Shui Sang Tseung, who began his career with the MTA as a chassis maintainer and mechanic in December of 1985 and worked until September, 9th 2001, when he became foreman, wrote, "As much as how the union claims they are doing everything to protect us from diesel fumes. They will not do anything that will shut a depot down. How hard is it to conduct an air sample test of a depot during the morning pull out?"

To this last point, several workers maintain they never saw air samples taken during the AM service, despite the fact that this is the time when workers on those shifts received the greatest exposure. One of my husband's close friends on the job, Joseph Covelli, wrote to me extensively about conditions in the garages. I've reproduced a large portion of what he wrote below, as I believe he fairly depicts conditions in the MTA garages during the time that my husband worked in them. He ends with an observation regarding how, or rather, when, air samples were taken:

> In regard to Tony's situation, he was exposed to a higher concentration of exhaust fumes than the average mechanic was. Tony mostly worked AM service, and that would entail breathing the fumes of the majority of the running buses that were being prepared to go out in the morning after sitting all night. Winter time was the worst situation, especially at Walnut Depot. The buses were parked outside overnight, and the depot was right on the river. The intense cold required that buses be running all night or they would not start in the morning. Industrial diesel engines do not have glow plugs to assist with starting, so you either ran the engines all night or you had to spray ether into the engine to start it in the AM.
>
> Either way, the resulting fumes that exited the engines after running them all night were excessive. The clouds of white smoke would hide a person only a few feet away from you. The other issue was the buses were then driven through the depot from the backyard in the morning and that also increased the exhaust exposure during AM service. That was the only way a bus could get to the front from the back yard.

Of course, electric trolleys don't need to run all night. He went on to write:

> Of all the occupations out there, I believe we were exposed to the most concentrations of hazardous materials

and exhaust concentrations. I use the word concentrations because you never had just one bus running at one time. There were many running at one time indoors, the concentration level definitely exceeded the minimal limited back then. However, as always, air samples were taken at the best of times and never in the evening or during AM service.

It seems obvious now that working day in, day out in an environment like that would cause health issues, but for so many years few people cared.

As to why the men worked under these conditions, Joseph also touched on that in his correspondence with me. He wrote:

What's interesting to note and what many don't know is that back then, this company was mainly run by first generation immigrant[s], that we[re] born on the "other side" as they use[d] to say.

I witnessed first-hand the mentality of "you're lucky you have a job", don't complain. Over there "we worked the fields or farm all day to earn a dollar". In the late 70's the laid off police and firemen were given jobs here. Again the "you're lucky if you have a job" mentality ruled. You could not rock the boat, as they say.

He continued:

We were exposed to a lot, we didn't have a choice or option other than to leave. Times were not good here in the US when I started here, the early 80's. I was laid off from a car dealer before I came here. At the time my wife was 8 months pregnant, I didn't have a choice I had to work. That was the case with many people here.

Finally, he wrote, "We were all exposed to a lot of issues here. When I started in 1982 there were no health warnings or safety guidelines, it wasn't mentioned or allowed. If you raised a concern you were simply told to leave."

Joseph Covelli has worked for the MTA for 35 years. He began having health problems, which started with asthma and developed into COPD in the last 8 years. He's now at 60% lung capacity and takes something like 8 pills a day, sleeps with a Bi-pap machine, and needs a nebulizer three times a day; he also has two stents in his heart. People always ask him how long he smoked, but the answer is, "never!" Joseph turned 60 in October of 2017 and has plans to retire at the age of 62.

As the 1980s turned into the 1990s, the company began to make efforts to clean up the air quality for the workers, or at least to make overtures in this direction. The workers also began to take note of the hazard, and as one of my husband's friends told me, workers complained enough that one shop steward actually called OSHA [Occupation Safety and Health Association] to request an air test. When OSHA arrived, they issued masks for the men to wear that also collected air quality samples. It's important to note that these masks would have taken samples during the AM service as well as for the entire period for which they were worn. After the samples were collected in a few days, the men in the garage were informed that air quality was at an acceptable level. This was in a location where the people working in the garage couldn't see from one side of the room to the other and mechanics and others needed to step outside from time to time for a breath of fresh air.

As the MTA, along with the Union, began to focus on air quality problems, one of the procedures they developed was a safety program. Once a week, foremen were supposed to hold safety meetings with their men, going over basic procedures. One of these procedures was to exhaust idling buses into hoses that diverted the fumes into a filtration system, which seems to have only pertained to buses that were undergoing maintenance in specific areas. If the procedure wasn't followed, the foremen was supposed to take action.

It appears, however, that this procedure, when implemented, was ineffective at best, and did not even apply to all of the buses in a garage. Furthermore, when the buses were running it would have been impossible to keep all, or even most of, the fumes out of the building. For instance, if there was oil on an engine and that engine was running, then the bus would produce a certain amount of smoke in the environment. In places like Walnut Street, as Joseph Covelli wrote, buses had to be driven through the garage from the back lot to the front for morning service. This is just a minor example of the difficulty of keeping these fumes out of the air, but the reality was far worse. There were as many as 325 buses at any given location, many of those were running inside, and buses seldom were hooked up to the exhaust and filtration system and couldn't be. As Tony Cunnane wrote:

> My dad was the Union Chairman in 100 ST and he retired in 1990. I remember that the hoses were in place during his tenure during the 80's but that was only on the maintenance lifts and specific areas where work was be[ing] done off the lifts. The real issues at 100 ST pertaining to smoke and fumes (I am speaking about the old 100 ST which closed in the late 90's) was morning service where when the buses were started and had low air, the shifters would just press the accelerator pedal to full throttle to raise the air pressure to operating level. The smoke would be so thick you could cut it with a knife, this would be the same in both levels of the building.

On the subject of exhausting buses indoors, Brian Brandwein, who worked the Gun Hill Depot, wrote: "I worked my last years at Gun Hill [in] 1997 and never saw them [buses] hooked up to the exhaust. I just remembered the only place I saw the exhaust hoses was the inspection area."

When asked about ventilation in the depots and garages, Andrew Mazzola wrote:

> I started at 100 ST in 1979. No exhaust. The building was falling down . . . Every garage except for Gunhill was a dungeon. As far as Gunhill I don't remember an exhaust system. I worked in every depot. Property protection . . .
>
> Let me tell you about Hudson Pier in winter. It was so cold all windows were closed. How about the order [that] all buses upstairs had to be left on so they could move them in morning. [sic] I had to walk around and check them. No hoses. Are you kidding me?

According to his testimony, and others, these buses ran, indoors, all night long without ventilation. Imagine what the air was like. The building was literally steeped in noxious fumes. The air was regularly so thick with exhaust that it was difficult to see. To this point, Tom C. Stentiford, who worked with Anthony in the 1980s, wrote:

> I started with Tony in 1982 at the old KB [Kingsbridge], there was no hoses for exhaust, no eye or ear protection and no gloves to be worn. The lower level in the morning would fill with smoke as the drivers/shifters built up the air making it hard to see and breathe. In the mid 80's I worked the equipment truck fixing the [hi-lows] and sweepers as Tony did, in the authorities garages and don't remember exhaust hoses in them. When the exhaust hoses appeared, the only policing of exhaust hoses came from the union reps and stewards who would shut down a bus if no hose was attached, me being one of the same.

To get some idea of how a garage operated, for instance, the 100th Street Depot had been built to house electric trolley cars. Part of the facility had been built in 1895 on the Lexington Avenue Line and then expanded to its final size in 1907. It was also a totally closed facility, and served both transportation and maintenance needs, and held about a hundred buses split over two floors inside. In preparation for the AM service, every bus was started in the early morning hours, and the fumes concentrated on the second floor.

At 100th Street, there was only one way in, through two giant old wooden doors on rollers that actually needed to be physically pushed back to open. Upon entering, on the left-hand side was the "chief's" office; the lifts were at the end, and to the right was another work area; from there, a ramp led to the second floor, which resembled a big warehouse, with a few pits for working under buses.

Making matters worse, the MTA was still using 2-Stroke, Detroit Diesel, Series 92 motors until the mid to late 1990s. According to what I've been told these motors used to smoke "like hell."

As to exhausting buses through hoses attached to the tail pipes: if and when it was used, that system was based on the exhaust running through filters; filters that also needed to be maintained on a regular basis. I mention this to point out how difficult it is to prepare and maintain hundreds of buses for daily AM and PM service while simultaneously protecting the people who work in and around the buses from the exhaust spewing all around them.

CHAPTER 10
TROLLEY CARS AND DIESEL BUSES

Whatever... When I've asked bus mechanics who worked in the old MTA trolley barns in New York City what happened to the electric trolley system, many told me that the rubber and oil companies had gotten rid of it in order to line their own pockets. When I first heard this explanation, I was skeptical. When I began to research it, however, I found a tremendous amount of data that backs it up.

Up until 1937, and a little later in the outer boroughs, New York City operated an extensive network of electric street rail cars - also known as trolleys. These ran on tracks called lines, powered by electricity conducted through overhead wires. But corporations like General Motors, with the help of local politicians, and Depression Era federal regulation, by and large phased the street rail cars out, removed the infrastructure, and began operating diesel buses in their place.

We know many of the nationwide aspects of the story from court proceedings. In the late 1940s, and after years of municipal street car track closures followed by a public campaign and the printing of a popular pamphlet by the founder of the Electric Railroaders' Association, Edwin J. Quinby, General Motors, Standard Oil of California, Firestone Tire, Phillips Petroleum, and Mack Truck were indicted in federal court in the case United States vs. National City Lines. National City Lines being the holding company through which the others operated. The indictment resulted in the 1949 conviction of the group for "Conspiring to monopolize sales of buses and supplies to companies owned by National City Lines." The consequence was a mere slap on the wrist.

Separately, in the same court case, the holding company and its principals were acquitted of attempting to monopolize transit ownership. But monopolizing industry ownership wasn't what the racket was after. It didn't matter who owned municipal transportation companies as long as that company purchased products from the companies behind National City Lines. As Quinby had argued in the pamphlet that helped bring about the trial, National City Lines had been engaged in a, "careful, deliberately planned campaign to swindle you out of your most important and valuable public utilities – your Electric Railway System."

The book *Internal Combustion,* by New York Times bestselling author Edwin Black, details much of this story in a chapter titled "The GM Conspiracy."

The book, published in 2006, is well researched and highly regarded, and exposes the profit motive behind the federally convicted conspirators in setting up National City Lines. In recognizing the fortune to be made by eliminating competition wherever possible, the group sought to establish local captive markets, ensuring that their products, the diesel bus, diesel fuel, rubber, etc., could not be rejected in favor of the less expensive, sturdier, and seemingly more popular trolley. Black notes that when Firestone Tire invested in National City Lines, they stipulated that in return, "all corporations and other entities which it [National City Lines] now controls . . . shall equip and shall continue to equip all their transportation units with Firestone products to the exclusion of any products competitive thereto . . ." (228)

When Phillips Petroleum joined the deal with National City Lines, lawyers added a clause to the contract, Clause 6, stipulating, that "the acquired transit systems never again use a non-petroleum based form of propulsion without Phillip's permission" (228).

A very big business, indeed. The group was responsible for the demise of large segments of LA's electric transit system and the permanent stripping of that part of its electric street car infrastructure. To this point, in the 1996 PBS documentary *Taken for a Ride - The U.S. History of the Assault on Public Transport in the Last Century*, producers interviewed Barney Larrick, former operation's manager for Pacific City Lines, a subsidiary of National City Lines, who helped dismantle much of L.A.'s street car system. When asked on camera if the systems were profitable before he was brought in, Larrick replied, "Well, after I got done chopping their heads off they didn't make money. Cut the miles down. Sell off their properties. Pull the company down."

In the same film, Jim Holzer, who was an L.A. railway worker, claims that Los Angeles had the finest public transportation system in the country before National City Lines spent a decade demolishing it.

In the widely circulated 1946 pamphlet, which helped raise public awareness about what National City Lines, et al., was then doing, and which helped to bring about the federal indictment, Edwin J. Quinby described three methods by which municipalities lost their electric rail systems. Of the third method he wrote, "The bus interests actually buy into the electric railway utility sufficiently to gain control—and then proceed to destroy the property in order to expand the market for their buses." And since the object was to sell more rubber, oil, and buses, it didn't matter whether an electric system disappeared overnight or over decades, as long as the interests were selling more of their goods.

Many people all over the country expressed dissatisfaction with the change in systems. Roger Arnebergh, who was, at the time of filming for *Taken for a Ride,* Los Angeles Assistant City Attorney, remembers how badly the new buses stank when they came on line. He claims they dramatically and noticeably added to the city's pollution. Edwin Black further writes that people in Lincoln, Nebraska followed the last run of their street car in a kind of sad procession throughout the city; even the dogs followed along. And one letter to the editor, also cited by Black, says, "The most cruel thing ever done was to take away the streetcars and give us these jolting buses that never take you where you want to go" (p. 237). Imagine what that letter to the editor would have said if the writer knew the buses also gave you cancer.

Prior to the creation of National City Lines, New York City's street rail lines had been demolished in a similar manner, and by many of the same players. However, the story of how and why New York City removed its electric street cars for diesel buses is not as clear cut as it is in a city like St. Petersburg, Florida, for instance, where city officials received Cadillacs before voting to scrap their electric rail system, or as it was in the case United States vs. National City Lines. Nevertheless, many signs of similar nefarious interference are also present.

Brad Snell, an attorney and one-time researcher at the Brookings Institute, has made the strongest argument in favor of a National City Lines style scheme operating in New York City in the 1920s and 30s to rid the city of its electric trolley system. He argues that the assault on Manhattan's transit system began when Alfred P. Sloan, the CEO of General Motors, bought "the largest bus-operating company in the country [Omnibus] and the largest production company [Yellow Coach] . . . [and] Between 1926 and '36 [GM] methodically destroyed the rails [in New York City]."

Edwin Black further described the impetus for General Motors
position against electric trolleys in the 1920s when he wrote, "In
the face of uncertainty about future automobile sales, GM decided
to branch into transit motor buses. The company was convinced it
could systematically convert thousands of electric transit systems
throughout the nation to oil burners" (206). And so it did.

However, General Motors could not have easily removed New
York City's surface rail if there had not already been a campaign
against the electric trolleys by none other than the mayor of New
York City, John S. Hylan. Nor could the rubber, oil, and bus interests have so quickly succeeded in converting New York's surface
rail to diesel buses without the Public Utility Holding Company
Act of 1935 which forced utility companies to separate from the
transit utilities they owned, making it more difficult to make a
profit. A decade after that law's enactment and the almost total
conversion of New York City to diesel, Edwin Quinby would ask
the question, "WHEN THE ELECTRIC RAILWAY IS FORCED
BY LAW TO BE SEPARATED FROM ITS POWER PLANT,
HOW CAN THE RESULTING SACRIFICE OF EFFICIENCY
AND ECONOMY POSSIBLY BENEFIT THE PUBLIC?" [caps in
original]

He further put his finger on the cause of the demise of the
New York system, and systems like it, when he wrote,

> The fact is that an electric railway which has been saddled
> with continually increasing taxes and increasing labor and
> maintenance material prices and which has been repeated-
> ly denied any increase in fare rates to compensate, might be
> just about able to continue to show a narrow margin of prof-
> it while supplied with power from its own plant at cost. But
> forced by law into separation from its power plant with the
> resultant higher costs for power, this electric railway might
> be driven into receivership and might quickly fall prey to

the depredations of the National City Lines-American City Lines clique[†].

In such an environment, General Motors was able to capitalize on local greed, corruption, political infighting, and New Deal legislation to help rid the city of its electric surface rail system and replace it with dirty-running diesel buses. Doing so effectively brought power generation for surface public transportation from offsite, large scale production facilities to inside the city at street level and even indoors alongside the people who operated and maintained the vehicles.

In 1985, when Anthony started working for the MTA, the buses were still leaving behind plumes of black smoke whenever they pulled away from stops, the garages were covered in soot, and so were the nearby buildings, which was an offense to both the transit workers and the nearby population.

The first offense, however, was to strip the electric street car grid out of cities big and small across the country. And the stripping of this infrastructure had an even more disastrous effect upon cities where electric surface rail had formed the back bone of public transportation and where other options were limited or not available, as in the above cited Lincoln, Nebraska. Given the environmental predicament in which we, as a society, currently find ourselves, an already existent, all-electric street car grid would be of great value today.

Compounding the problem, when New York City switched from electric trolleys to diesel buses, the city also continued using the electric trolley garages, called barns, as depots. They neglected, at that time, and for decades afterward, to adjust the structure of the garages to accommodate the needs of those who worked in, on, or near the pollution-emitting buses. But trolleys don't burn fuel and exhaust carcinogens, they also don't idle indoors, and so

---

[†] American City Lines merged with National City Lines in 1946.

don't pollute the indoor air quality as diesel engines do. In other words, they don't poison you. And while power generation itself, typically coal generated in the United States, is not pollution free, the electric trolleys that utilize this energy have the benefit of not exhausting directly into streets and garages, a problem that was exponentially worse in the 20th century, but continues to be an issue today.

Although the federal government and the MTA have made efforts to reduce diesel emissions and improve air quality in the last ten years, it's not clear to what extent new workers remain exposed to the fumes, or how the company intends to address the effects of diesel emissions on those workers whose careers preceded, or partially preceded, the recent reduction in emissions.

As to exposure levels endured by mechanics, according to a literature review conducted by Anjoeka Pronk, Joseph Coble, and Patricia A. Stewart, and found in the *Journal of Exposure Science and Environmental Epidemiology* (2009), available at Nature.com, "Exposure levels of miners and underground construction workers were highest (154–1600 and 121 $\mu g/m^3$, respectively), followed by mechanics, above-ground construction workers, and taxi drivers." But exactly how those exposure levels have affected, and continue to affect, cancer rates at the MTA, and how they break down by garages and positions, isn't yet known.

Even if they were, statistics could never tell the full story. I spent years attending the diesel fume forums and conducting my own research to try to understand. I saw Anthony and his friends in those reports, talks, and papers, and I knew what happened to them. But why, if it was now so obvious to everyone, to me, to the workers, to the scientists, doctors, and lawyers what had happened, why hadn't the early death of so many MTA employees ever made news before? How could it remain an open secret for so long?

We live in one of the most renowned cities in the world, a city that in certain ways looks down its nose at other parts of the country; at, for instance, places like West Virginia where men die from their occupation in the coal mines. But we never imagined that we have our very own coal miners right in the streets, tunnels, and garages of Manhattan, dying from something as simple as the exhaust from buses.

Now, whenever I see a bus, I can't help but think that someone at that very moment is getting sick from inhaling its fumes inside the bowels of a city that should know better, and should have known better for generations. And it's my goal to make others see it too.

The more I came to know about the link between diesel fumes and cancer, the angrier I got, and the more determined I became to expose it.

CHAPTER 11
CARCINOGENIC TO HUMANS

On June 12th, 2012, a few months after I joined John Dearie's lawsuit, we heard that the World Health Organization had declared that diesel fumes were a Group 1 carcinogen.

"It's about time," I thought.

The WHO had studied the relationship between diesel and cancer for 50 years and finally decided that those fumes were carcinogenic, rather than just "probably" carcinogenic, as defined in their former 2A classification. I can't imagine how it could take 50 years to come up with a definitive answer. It's not that complicated.

In Mark Twain's day, his mother knew that smoking wasn't good for your health. She didn't need a panel of government scientists and a 50-year study to tell her so. Likewise, the MTA wouldn't need a panel of scientists to tell them that letting their people work inside of garages full of diesel fumes was bad for them. They would certainly not have needed it after years of watching those same people come down with cancer and die. And after paying for the cancer treatment, for the MTA to pretend like they couldn't know what was happening is beyond the pale.

The recent scientific consensus and the 50 years it took to get there offer cover for the culpable parties to claim that the so-called "science" had not yet established a definitive link between diesel fumes and cancer. Surely, however, an analysis of their own records would have explained what was happening. The old question asked by Senator Howard Baker during Watergate seems to be the crux of the matter with regard to diesel fumes, cancer, and the 2012 declaration by the WHO: "What did the president know, and when did he know it." It seems science says that we didn't know until 2012, but that is absurd. The employee' records and data collected by companies like the MTA are scientifically valid after all and always would have been.

The fact is, full-emission diesel buses exhausting fumes into garages where people work causes cancer. The MTA would have known it as soon as they started paying for employee medical expenses, and as soon as the company began tracking employee longevity rates.

Whether records exist, and weren't destroyed is another matter. To suspend the declaration of diesel as a carcinogen until 2012, while a step in the right direction, is a public relations absolution with possible legal consequences for the companies previous to 2012, since it can be argued that the link between cancer and diesel fumes wasn't definitively established; the science wasn't *in* so to speak.

My suspicions about the MTA's knowledge and use of its employees' health issues is exemplified by the following story. One of my husband's friends who also worked for the MTA wasn't feeling well. He went to the doctor who diagnosed him with hepatitis C. Given his lack of other potential exposure to the virus, he concluded that it must have come from contact with bodily fluids he encountered while working on the buses. In particular, he believed he contracted it while doing maintenance work on the handicapped ramps because they are often used as toilets. Within a year of his diagnosis, the MTA sent out form letters to everyone in the company who worked on buses. It described how to avoid contracting hepatitis while working on the buses.

It certainly wasn't his particular case that caused the MTA to send the letter to so many of its employees. Rather, it appears the company had discovered a trend in its worker population and was making employees aware of the dangers to lessen their exposure to the disease. Whether hepatitis C had infected five, fifty, or fifty-thousand workers, the MTA had recognized an illness that posed a threat to its people and responded. How could they not have noticed cancer among the population, or noticed which employees did and did not tend to get sick?

All this is by way of explaining that there is no way in the world the New York MTA, or companies like it, didn't know that their workers were getting sick and dying from cancer. The pattern would have been abundantly evident in a company that treats its workers as numbers. They didn't need the WHO to tell them so.

Despite what I'm now writing about the WHO's decision, I was happy that it unequivocally signaled that I wasn't alone in my conviction that diesel fumes cause cancer, nor was I the only one becoming vocal about this issue. And I believed that their decision boded well for our own lawsuit.

The next week, however, we learned that John Dearie had lost; and he had lost based on wording in the Clean Air Act, an act which gave cover to engine manufacturers for the very thing we were suing them for. As the letter, sent on July 19, 2012, from John Dearie stated,

In summary, the Federal Court of Appeals, Second Circuit, three judge panel sitting in New York City heard Oral Arguments last month and interpreted Congressional intent in the Clean Air Act to exclude (preclusion) any lawsuit like ours.

Our case rested on two theories; First – fuel emission standards; and second – failure by the engine manufacturers to warn of the dangers from exposure to diesel exhaust. By the Court's Decision, regrettably the case never progressed to the trial stage where we would have advanced the argument about prolonged exposure causing medical illnesses and disease.

This meant, in my mind at least, that the Clean Air Act had been written as much to protect corporations as it had been to keep the air clean. Perhaps rather than the Clean Air Act, it should have been titled the Acceptable Levels of Pollution Act; or the Corporate Emissions Protection Act.

We had lost on a technicality written into legislation to defend the polluters themselves.

I was later to learn that losing on such a basis isn't unheard of. Legislation passed, in theory, to protect people's health, is and can be used to circumvent the defense of it. What I was learning about the way America worked truly shocked me. It seemed I was constantly being reminded of the Soviets back in Poland, except here the totalitarian schemes had corporate faces.

I don't think I sat around feeling sorry for myself for very long after we lost Dearie's case. I couldn't turn back now, after all that I had learned since my husband's death.

I didn't know what to do, however. It appeared that the United States had long ago erected barriers to prevent anyone from winning this kind of case.

On the other hand, I believed that all these people's deaths had to mean something, and I knew that the WHO's proclamation that diesel fumes cause cancer would have consequences in the United States. And yet even though it seemed so clear to me that we had a winning argument, I just didn't know how to pursue it.

It was a few weeks after the Dearie trial, in August of 2012, when a friend of Anthony's called me to ask how I was doing. After listening to me talk about the failure of our civil suit, he suddenly said, "You should bring a workers' compensation lawsuit," and since he had been working in and around this topic for years, he knew where to go, "Grey and Grey," he said, and gave me their information.

I was happy to hear it. I had been thinking in this direction for a few days, but hadn't landed on a way to get it started.

As it turned out, Grey and Grey LLP had offices in Manhattan and in Farmingdale, NY not far from my home. I drove to the Farmingdale office the following day where I met with attorney Alissa Gardos. I gave her all the information I had. She was kind, but she was also careful and a little skeptical.

"Do you have any documentation?" She asked.

Of course I did.

I had kept every piece of paper I had received from Anthony's company, and anything he had on file as well as what I had gotten from the hospitals and doctors. As of that point, and even though I had done the partial autopsy, I couldn't get anyone to test the tissue samples to see what exactly they contained, and so I couldn't use those then. On this note: I've asked hospitals and research facilities across the country to test my husband's tissues (which I had had preserved) and all have since declined.

Alisa agreed to speak further with me after she had a chance to review my documents, which I sent her the following day. After she got a look at them, she gave me a call, and was happy to talk with me. The lawyers at Grey and Grey now thought that we had a case that we could win. At that point, we moved forward, although it felt like it was going in slow motion.

At the same time, I continued attending the forums both in Manhattan and in Brooklyn.

While I had learned a great deal from the people there, it seemed as though we weren't going to change anything. I wanted to learn how to turn our community of diesel fume victims into a real force for change. How could there be so much evidence making the connection between diesel fumes and cancer, and yet no one could make any headway?

The pace at which my suit was moving was also beginning to wear on me. It wasn't until a year later, in October of 2013, that we had our first hearing.

I took time off that day to be at the hearing, but when I arrived Grey and Grey had sent a lawyer I had never met before. What followed was a disaster. My lawyer actually came unprepared. He hadn't studied the case, and didn't know the facts. I could have done a better job on my own. At this point I was new to courtrooms and hearings before judges, so I didn't know what to expect. One thing I did know was that you didn't show up to court unprepared.

I left the hearing furious and called Grey and Grey immediately. I got through to Brian O'Keefe, who was one of the more senior attorneys in the firm.

"Enough's enough," I said. "You sent me a lawyer fresh out of law school who just embarrassed me in front of the MTA lawyer – in front of the judge. This is not a joke to me. I'm not going to put up with it. If you're going to jerk me around, then I'm going with someone else."

Brian apologized and promised to send a different attorney in the future. They took me more seriously after that. But that didn't mean that things were moving any faster. And I was growing tired.

I continued to attend the forums because I thought something might come of them, but at a certain point, I had heard everything they had to say. Here and there someone might have discussed an interesting point or two, but none of that was getting anything done.

And then it happened.

In the Spring of 2013, I found myself sitting in the wrong place at the New York Committee for Occupational Safety & Health

(NYCOSH) forum on Diesel Fumes and Lung Cancer. It wasn't clear to me in which office the talks were being held, and I entered a smaller room where a panel convened for a limited audience of insiders. Several doctors and scientists were speaking. I considered leaving the room when one of my husband's friends got up and spoke about diesel and ventilation in the garages. He also mentioned my husband and the type of work he did, and how he was exposed to diesel fumes and had recently died of cancer.

Maybe it was because I knew the man, or maybe it was because he mentioned my name; whatever the reason, when he finished speaking, I took advantage of the opportunity and spoke up.

"My name's Dorota Nigro," I said suddenly, as I stood from my chair. Everyone in the room turned to look at me. "I was the wife of Anthony Nigro." I continued, "My husband worked for the MTA for 28 years as a diesel engine mechanic. He did the AM service and was exposed to fumes for 4-5 hours each morning.

"As I'm sure you can hear, I speak with an accent," I said. "I'm Polish. My husband was of Italian descent. We have two children who we raised to be good American citizens. We taught them not to be passive, but to take action for what they believe, and that's what I'm trying to do here. I've been to half-a-dozen of these conventions. I've seen many of you before, but what I don't understand is how, for all the talk, nothing ever gets done; in a city of this size we need to take action.

"I became an American citizen 40 years ago, but now, for the first time, I feel embarrassed to admit that I'm an American. On June 12, 2012 after 50 years of research, the World Health Organization just declared that diesel fumes cause lung cancer. But a week afterward our federal courts turned down a lawsuit against the diesel engine companies.

"It's embarrassing to call ourselves the greatest country in the world when we can't, or won't, do anything about this. How long are we just going to talk about it? It's common sense that diesel fumes cause lung cancer. If anybody doesn't believe that, then maybe they should lay down behind a bus and inhale for a while.

"Because of the damage to workers from bus fumes, the MTA's failure to improve ventilation in their depots has been extraordinarily negligent. Some of the old garages, the so-called "trolley barns," had no ventilation at all for years. Other garages have ventilation but they don't change the filters on the systems as frequently as they need to, and the walls on the lower levels of the garages are so black from fumes they need to be power-washed once a month. Soot that settles on the walls is so thick you can scrape it with a knife.

"I spent just 15 minutes in the newer garage on 41st where my husband used to work, and that's supposed to be clean, but in that time I could taste the particles of diesel in my mouth.

"We live in a city where 12 million people are exposed to diesel fumes every day and have been for generations. That's just a fraction of the people across the country affected by this. Don't you see that all the people who have been hurt by diesel fumes are the greatest support we could have in this fight – if we would only start acting to organize people and inform them instead of just talking about it?"

At that point, the different journalists who were in the room suddenly started to pay attention to me. A few of the ones in my vicinity introduced themselves and handed over their business cards. The gentleman who had been sitting directly in front of me also turned and looked at me. He smiled and said, "I'm Brian O'Keefe of Grey and Grey. I'm your lawyer."

"Fancy meeting you here." I said.

He smiled again.

As the forum went back to normal, Brian and I talked for a bit, but it was difficult to have a close conversation in that atmosphere and so he asked me to meet him later in his office. After we agreed on a date and time, the forum broke up and we went our separate ways. As I left, Sarah Dorsey, who wrote for The Chief Leader, a civil service newspaper in Manhattan, approached me. I met with her again not long after that near the Michael Quill garage in Midtown where Anthony used to work. She later quoted me in a March 11, 2013 article for The Chief, and wrote several follow up articles on our progress with the lawsuit.

A few days after I spoke out at the forum I met Brian in Farmingdale. After some pleasantries, I again expressed how dissatisfied I was with both the course of the case and the lawyer they had sent to the first hearing. He apologized again. "I'm not in this case to lose it," I said, "I'm a sore loser."

"I understand."

We talked a bit more about how we were going to proceed and then he got to the business he had asked me there for in the first place.

"I want you to *lay* low," he said.

"If you want me to *lay* low, you'd better start working on the case."

He promised me he would, and I promised to do as he said.

Around the same time that I went to meet with Brian O'Keefe, I received a call from some of my husband's former coworkers in the MTA letting me know that the Transit Authority wasn't happy with what I had said – they weren't happy with my outspoken personality. Too bad.

"Really," I said, "tell them I'd like to meet them for a cup of coffee in Manhattan on Saturday or Sunday, and we can compare who is more upset. You can tell them also, to stay the f**k out of my way." Nothing ever came of that, of course.

At least they knew who I was, and what I thought. I wasn't about to stand down. I might be quiet for a while, but that was only because I believed my lawyers were speaking and working on my behalf and that our lawsuit was proceeding. As I waited, I did everything I could do to help. The most useful thing that I did was to give the lawyers the records we had kept from the MTA and from the hospitals and doctors Anthony had been to.

The hearings continued, and at each one a new hearing would be scheduled. Nothing seemed to actually take place, but then Alissa Gardos got the MTA's doctor to admit there was a possibility that the diesel fumes in the garages contributed to my husband's cancer. I started to think we were getting somewhere.

From that point forward, it seemed the hearings came one after the other. We had about five of them in a row. The most memorable were the last two.

In the first of those hearings, I found that couldn't hold my tongue. I couldn't "lay" low. I spoke up when the MTA's lawyer actually asked the question, "How do we know how much Anthony was exposed to diesel?"

"Are you kidding me?" I blurted, "He did AM service."

Judge Leibowitz replied, "Mrs. Nigro, please. You need to control yourself."

"Sorry." I said, but it was just such a stupid question that I couldn't help but have a bit of an outburst.

But a strange thing happened because I spoke up; at that moment, the MTA lawyer looked at me and asked, "What's AM service?" Apparently, he was a less astute attorney than my previous one, and hadn't done his homework either. How could he possibly work on this case on behalf of the MTA, in which knowing what my husband did, where, and when were the critical facts?

"You're the MTA lawyer, and they didn't brief you on my husband's job description? Shame on you, I rest my case."

I looked at Judge Leibowitz. He didn't seem amused, "I always wanted to say that," I said, and shrugged my shoulders. "May I explain it, Please?"

The judge gave me permission to speak, and I explained my husband's job as an MTA mechanic for AM service.

I told him how Anthony left home at 4:00 AM to start his job at 4:50 in Manhattan. There he released 200 to 300 buses onto the streets of New York to make the morning service.

"For a mechanic," I said, "the AM service begins in preparing the buses for the day. A lot of those buses have minor problems that can be solved more or less on the spot. Anthony and the other mechanics would get them ready.

"And getting the buses ready all happens while the dispatcher is dispatching them and while the buses are idling. Some of the buses are in the garage while others are out in the parking lot. If a blinker light is out, for instance, then Anthony would go and fix the light while the bus idles. And Diesel buses are always idling, especially in winter. They idle nonstop, all the while they're spitting heavy fumes.

"The AM service ran from the time Anthony arrived to about 8:30 in the morning, and all that time those buses were running. The buses also exhaust thicker diesel fumes as they leave the depot, and as they accelerate up the ramp and out of the garage they leave a cloud of fumes that my husband and other mechanics, bus drivers, and sweepers inhaled. That's AM service and that's what he did for the last 8 years of his life. Do you think his exposure to diesel fumes was sufficient to develop lung cancer? A cancer that surfaced as stage-four inoperable without any warning?"

I stopped there, but I could have kept going. Judge Leibowitz thanked me and excused us.

From there on out I knew we were going to win the case. In fact, I had believed we were going to win from the very first day I had laid eyes on the judge. I just had a very strong feeling about it. I thought he was honest, and any honest assessment of my case would come out in my favor.

In the final hearing, three of my husband's former co-workers testified for us. They had all been Anthony's friends; two had been his bosses and one a partner. It was important that they were retired; people still working for the MTA were, at least from what I'd witnessed, unlikely to speak as they feared reprisals from the company. Each witness testified separately. The questions asked of them were the same and their answers were consistent.

The MTA lawyers called a single witness, one with whom a pre-arranged call had been scheduled to allow him to testify by speakerphone from his work location.

In due course, the call was placed to the MTA's witness's workplace. A secretary answered the phone. Her response to the judges request to talk to the witness was heard throughout the courtroom: "No, he's not here," she said, "He took a vacation day."

And that was that.

After that, the case came up for the judge to decide. My lawyers were nervous then, but after the judge had allowed me to speak and to nearly embarrass the other lawyer, and since the defense's witnesses failed to show up for court, I couldn't see how we could lose.

Judge Leibowitz took a week to make up his mind. We won –the victory, however, came with several caveats. One of these was that rather than receiving a lump sum award, I would get paid in fixed monthly instalments, which was specified by a New York State law that determined how workers' compensations awards are paid out. My lawyers, on the other hand, did get a lump sum. There was a further stipulation, which was that I couldn't get remarried or I would lose the payout.

After I was informed of these limitation in court, I asked the judge if I could summarize the results of the decision. The judge agreed.

"So, my children lost their father. I lost my husband, and if I leave this room and get hit by a car I've lost everything I won. If I remarry, I lose the payments two years after that. Is that correct?" I said rhetorically. The judge nodded, and I said, "And I'll have to look at those MTA checks for the rest of my life and be reminded of what happened. I guess now I understand where the saying comes from, 'the first time for love, the second for money.' You'll make a good Catholic girl live in sin."

Judge Leibowitz laughed when I said that, but I wasn't finished, "The law is designed for lawyers. They get their money and I'm a schmuck the second time around. There are rules and regulations for the little people and another set for the big people to do whatever they want to do. Do I have that about right?"

Judge Leibowitz conceded that I did.

Brian O'Keefe looked at me then, "You won, he said. "You brought us the whole case on a silver platter. What did you need us for?"

"To keep the paperwork in order," I replied. He smiled at that, and we shook hands and went our separate ways.

I left the hearing and walked out of the courthouse where I looked to the sky and said, "I told you, Anthony, I'd win. It won't bring you back, but you're not just a number."

The written text of the decision came by mail from the State of New York – Workers Compensation Board.

In regard to Anthony Nigro (Dec'd), WCB Case #G059 6367. The Notice of Decision read:

At the Workers' Compensation hearing held on 06.09.2014 involving the claim of Anthony Nigro (Dec'd) at the Hempstead hearing location, Judge Jay Leibowitz made the following decision, findings and direction:

Decision: the claimant Anthony Nigro (Dec'd) had a work related injury from inhalation of diesel fumes that resulted in his death. The employer witness did not appear. The employer is precluded from producing witness(es).

Based upon the testimony and evidence in the record, the decedents exposure to diesel fumes at work played a part in his death. Dorota Nigro is the surviving spouse of the deceased...

The MTA had one month to appeal the decision. My lawyers were certain they would do so because allowing this award to stand would set a precedent that could prove extraordinarily costly to the MTA over time. I, on the other, felt very strongly that we had won outright and that the MTA and their attorneys wouldn't fight us any further. It was only right. Their medical report was weak and the lack of witnesses made their case even weaker. But aside from what I thought, I just had a feeling that was it.

In fact, the MTA did not appeal.

We had won the first compensation lawsuit in the state of New York and the first in the country where diesel was determined to have caused lung cancer.

I thought at that point that my fight was over, but I very soon realized that it had only just begun.

CHAPTER 12
BURIAL AT SEA

I learned that the MTA would not appeal the case by letter on July 29th, 2014. This was an important day for me for another reason as well.

While I was in India for work, Samantha had an accident. A group of her friends picked her up in a convertible Camero with the T-Tops down to take her to a pool party. She got into the front passenger seat. Two boys sat in the back. The boy who was driving, left our neighborhood and pulled onto Division Road at a high rate of speed. He was showing off and driving too fast and wasn't watching where he was going. Samantha, who saw that they were racing toward a parked truck, began screaming; somehow, the boy didn't see it. He crashed into the back of the truck, and the Camaro turned and slid alongside it before eventually coming to a stop.

Sam didn't have her seatbelt on, and they hit the truck with such force that she was ejected through the open T-Top and out onto the street where she bounced onto someone's lawn. They found her there, unconscious. The two passengers in the rear seat were fine, but the driver had his arm pinched between the truck and the Camero and needed skin grafts.

Three or four ambulances rushed to the accident and closed the road. Michael just happened to be coming home at that time. He saw the ambulances but couldn't get close enough to see what was going on. When he got home, his phone rang; one of his friends told him what happened to Sam. He rushed to the hospital, ready for the worst, but found Sam sitting up in bed with only scratches on her arm.

If you believe in that kind of thing, you might think that somebody was looking out for her. Who that was, I don't know, but I've had more and more encounters with coincidences that don't feel coincidental in recent years.

Mary left a message on my phone telling me what had happened. As I was returning from India at the time, I only heard it after I landed. As I always do, I checked my calls as soon as I could and heard Mary say, "Everything's all right." At that moment, I knew that something was very wrong. "Sam's had an accident," she said, and went on to tell me where my daughter was.

I rushed out of the airport as fast I could, leaving behind my in-flight shoes and apron as I went.

By the time I got to Long Island, she was already home, and when I came in she was sitting on the bed in perfect condition just looking at me. I wasn't sure if I wanted to kill her or hug her. I went with the latter. I was so grateful and relieved to see that she was ok; simultaneously, given my fears when I heard the message, I was rather shocked to see what good condition she was in. It gave me a strange feeling to see her there almost untouched by injury, after ejecting through the small T-Top opening of the Camero, landing and bouncing off Division Road and onto a lawn. We all thought her lack of injury was strange, to say the least. What it meant I didn't know, but there was more strangeness to come.

A month after Sam's accident, on September the 4th, I got a phone call from a Wall Street Journal reporter, Kris Mahr, who wanted to interview me about the case. I agreed, and they came and asked me questions and took pictures.

The next day, Saturday, that same reporter from the Journal called me and let me know that the article had run in the weekend edition.

I was excited to see it, and so I got into my car and drove to the nearby 7-Eleven to pick up a copy. On the way into the store I spotted a woman staring at me. I passed by her without another thought. Inside, I picked up two copies so I could give one to my sister who was staying at my house at the time. But something strange happened to me at the 7-Eleven, the memory of which would continually resurface in my mind, often giving me a little confidence when I needed it or prodding me along in those times where I felt like not doing anything.

As I passed by the woman on my way out the door, she addressed me. "Can I talk to you outside?" She said.

"Is something wrong? Can I help you?"

"I have very strong vibes about you."

"That's nice," I said, not really sure where this was going.

"You are very strong and very determined and you're going to be very successful in the future."

"I wish I was successful 30 years ago." I said, and laughed a little as I thanked her, "Maybe we'll see each other again sometime."

I walked out to my car trying to figure out what the heck just happened. I only believe what I see, but I had been seeing some things that felt unbelievable of late. As strange as it may sound, the lady at the 7-Eleven, and what she said, stayed with me. I told my sister and daughter about it, but they just rolled their eyes. I rolled them too, but again and again the memory of what she said would creep into my head.

But this was just a warmup to more, and stranger, events. My experience with the lady in 7-Eleven was just another signpost along the way; there would be more.

I went into Sam's room one morning to find her sitting up in bed.

"Dad was just here," she said.

"What do you mean?"

"I realize I was dreaming, but it was real."

She went on to describe what had happened. She said she was standing on a street that she'd never been on before. It had a row of houses close together and she thought that it was in Staten Island. A few houses down from her she saw her two cousins walk out of a front door. They were dressed in black and entered a black car, which headed off down the road. At that moment, she realized they were going to a funeral.

With that, Sam started walking toward the house her cousins had just walked out of. The house was narrow, brown, and brick and had a few steps leading up to the porch. She approached and climbed the porch stairs. For some reason, as she got close to the door leading into the house, she realized that she knew the layout of the home inside without entering. Instead of going in, she remained on the porch and looked around. To her left sat a small wooden table on which lay two Mass cards. Looking down at them, she didn't recognize one of the cards, but next to that was Anthony's card. She reached out and picked it up to look at it. As she was doing so, over her shoulder, she heard her dad's voice say, "It's someone they work with, they're going today to pay their respects." He was referring to the funeral.

When she got to this part of the story Sam said, "When I turned around I saw him standing there looking at me, only he didn't look the way he did when he passed. He looked healthy and happy. Not as old as 57, maybe a little younger, but still the same, but without as big of a belly and a touch less of a full head of gray."

He then said to her, "I know Rosemary's thinking of me today so I came to be with her. She thinks of me often."

Rosemary was his cousin who was attending the funeral of a friend.

At that point, he and Sam turned and walked down the stairs together and headed for the corner of the block, following the black car. They walked down the street without saying much. Sam remembered being happy, like they were almost laughing about something as they went. Then, in front of them in the distance, the cemetery where the black car had gone came into focus.

From there Sam said, "We started to turn the corner and he started walking across the street away from me. I followed behind him saying, 'where are you going . . . I miss you.'"

Her voice got shaky at that point and she was becoming choked up. She said she begged him, "Please don't go."

Tears started falling down her face then and he turned back and said, "Sam, you know I can't stay."

She felt he was getting upset, and he turned away and she fell to her knees hysterically crying. Looking up, she saw him walking into a white *aura* – something, as she described, like you see in the movies when a person walks into heaven with nothing behind them but a white glare.

He faded away just as she woke up sitting in bed. Her face was wet from tears. "I have this uneasy feeling that it wasn't just a dream; like someone's been in my room with me."

Sam's father had died. My husband had died. We were taking the loss as best we could, but the feeling of it never went away. People dream of loved ones all the time. Sometimes those dreams are more real than others. The strangest part of Sam's dream was first, how shaken up she had been, which gave me goose bumps, and second the fact that she had mentioned and described her second cousin Rosemary's house and a funeral in Staten Island. I knew she had never been to Rosemary's.

My daughter doesn't make up stories, she's like me, very fact based, and so I decided to call Rosemary to ask her if she had been to a funeral. Rosemary wasn't home when I called, so I talked to her sister Christine. "Yes," she said. "Rosemary's friend had died." Then I described her house as Sam had told me it looked, which it turns out was exactly what Rosemary's house looked like. I don't know what it means, but it gave me a chill up my spine to know that Sam had described two things she had no way of knowing from a dream where she talked with her father.

It would have been easy to say these experiences had no meaning, that they weren't real, or were induced by stress and loss, but there's more to life than that. Furthermore, Anthony always believed in destiny. He thought it was his to die. He had worked, taken care of his family, and it was his time to go. At the end, and when he was diagnosed, he accepted his fate. His acceptance was why he was able to die with such grace, and his acceptance came from the belief in destiny.

I had never had as strong a belief in destiny as Anthony did, and yet I couldn't shake the feeling that it was mine to expose the awful crime that a group of major companies has committed against their workers by, first, removing the electric trolley cars, and second, taking their diesel buses indoors without protecting employees. By doing this, these companies, along with our government, created and enabled a legacy of cancer.

Even though I had won the first compensation case linking diesel fumes to cancer, thereby setting a precedent, I felt that I had much more to do. At the same time, though, I wasn't sure how to move forward. This is where the universe, or whatever you believe provides moments of guidance, prompted me in the right direction. My upcoming high school reunion would oddly come to help me understand just how I might proceed. In January of 2013, a year after Anthony died, I received a letter. At first glance I thought it was from Anthony's high school, "Oh, God," I thought, "Now I have to call his school and let them know what happened." But I opened the envelope and found a letter inviting me to my reunion. I wondered why they were sending the notification so far in advance of the event. At first, I didn't want anything to do with the reunion. I had barely spoken the language when I first came here, and had hardly made a single friend there. But as time passed, I got more interested in seeing my old classmates. In addition, since the date was so far in the future, it occurred to me that by then I might want to go and start fresh, and so I sent them a check.

I also connected with one of my classmates on Facebook who was organizing the event. Her name was Helen Yee. She was very popular in high school. I had taken Russian classes with her and remembered her well. She remembered me also. Her mother was Polish and her father Chinese, so we had a nationality in common.

At first, we just talked on Facebook, but then we arranged to meet in Manhattan. I was in the city dropping off my passport for renewal. We had breakfast together and took a walk by the Gracie Mansion. It was nice to spend the day with someone from the past, and I was surprised at how quickly we became comfortable with each other. Interestingly, this rekindled friendship would, a few months later, provide further motivation for me to expose the devastating effects of diesel fumes.

My 40th high school reunion came on the 20th of September 2014. By then, I was looking forward to going back to New Jersey. About a 120 people showed up for the event, which was a good number. I had attended Dumont high school for just a year-and-a-half, and had kept in contact with no one from the graduating class, but I was looking at the reunion as a new start for me. I even planned to stay over at the hotel where the reunion was being hosted.

The first day of the reunion went well. I enjoyed the time because I wasn't focused on the MTA and Anthony's death.

We drank and danced. It seemed to me everyone had a good time, and I tried to ask a lot of questions so the conversations centered on other people. I didn't want to talk about what I had been going through. I wanted a new start, but I should have known it was impossible now.

Helen was great and introduced me to many of the people I had gone to school with but didn't really know at the time. They all said they remembered me; who knows if they really did. Helen went on to introduce me to Dr. Steven Stylianos, who worked at Columbia Presbyterian in the city. He told me his wife was Polish, and I asked him if she was "*Polish Polish*," or just "American Polish." He laughed, and said, "American Polish." I kept asking him questions, in part as a defense because I didn't want to focus the attention on myself and have the talk turn to what happened. I couldn't keep him from asking me questions forever, however, and at one point he stopped and said, "It's enough about me. Are you married, do you have kids? What about your husband, what does he do?

"Well, he's not around anymore," I said. He looked like he wanted more of an explanation, and so I decided to tell him about the story.

"I lost my husband to diesel fumes." I said. "He got lung cancer working for the MTA as a diesel mechanic, and I won the first compensation lawsuit in the country linking diesel fumes to cancer, about a month ago."

He looked shocked when I said that. "I have to give you a hug," he said. "You don't know how long we've been waiting for this."

I felt a little awkward, but I smiled. His hug justified one of my basic beliefs about diesel fumes and the cancer they cause. I knew that there had to be so many people suffering the effects of these fumes, along with their families, that many others had to understand what was going on as well. After all, for years, people pretended that cigarettes didn't cause cancer. Even while this subterfuge remained effective, many doctors who dealt with cancer cases couldn't help but recognize, sooner or later, that smoking was often the cause. With diesel it would've been the same. But there had been such an odd silence around diesel that speaking out could make you feel uneasy and alone.

Dr. Kessler, who was so knowledgeable and had been so honest with us before Anthony's death, certainly wasn't the only man in the world who had seen and read enough to know that diesel caused cancer even before the so-called "science" was in on the fact. I was happy to know that there were others. I took this as another sign that, not only was I on the right track, but that I had to keep going.

However, my talk with Dr. Stylianos wasn't the only encounter I'd have that linked back to my husband's cancer and the environment that gave it to him. I just couldn't escape it.

The next morning, I was ready to leave early. I showered, got dressed, and, after packing my stuff, I went downstairs to get a cup of coffee for the ride home. As I entered the restaurant, I noticed about twenty people sitting around the large table. They saw me as I passed by, and suddenly someone said, "Where do you think you're going? Get over here and have breakfast with us."

"Good morning," I said, looking over the group of classmates at the table. "I guess I have no choice."

I made my way toward the table and someone pulled out a chair for me. I sat down and people introduced themselves. Everyone was so warm and inviting.

Across from me sat a lady named Mary Marino. She was a nurse. I said hello and introduced myself. Then, within a minute of my sitting, one of Mary's friends, seated down the table from her, asked Mary something that led to a conversation I never expected. "Mary," she said, "How's your mother, did she ever remarry after your father passed away?"

"No, she didn't." Mary replied. "And I can't believe you remember that. It's been 22 years." Then Mary said, "My father worked for MTA." I practically spilled my coffee; my heart jumped, I wondered if I'd heard her right, but Mary continued, "He used to come home after work smelling like diesel fumes. My mother would wash his uniforms, and I remember how the inside of the washing machine would be black when she was done. There was a greasy slick that had to be removed after his clothes were washed." I couldn't believe what I was hearing. If I hadn't decided to come and get a cup of coffee, I would never have heard this. She continued. "He worked the trolley garages full of diesel fumes. He inhaled them all day long. When he died, I knew I should have pursued it legally with the MTA, but my family stopped me. I didn't do anything. But I still think about it."

My jaw was practically on the floor at this point. I tried not to say anything because I went to that reunion just to have a good time, but this was the first occasion in two-and-a-half years, outside of my own lawsuit, that I had heard a person mention trolley garages. I couldn't keep quiet.

"Mary, which part of the MTA did your father work for?"

She looked at me and said without hesitation, "MaBSTOA."

I quickly replied, "Manhattan and Bronx Surface Transit Operating Authority, and your father passed away from lung cancer."

She looked at me in surprise, "How do you know that?"

"My husband worked for MaBSTOA and passed away from lung cancer two-and-a-half years ago. I pursued it legally against MTA for their negligence."

It got quiet around us then. Suddenly everybody focused on me. I just looked at her, "I didn't want to bring this up here. I came to get away from it, but I haven't heard anybody talk about those things." I saw tears in Mary's eyes, and I realized again how many people had lost spouses and parents. They all still remember their losses, like I do. After so many years it doesn't go away; it never goes away, and we know that diesel caused our loved ones' deaths, and we know that the company understood the environmental peril they put their employees in and yet continued to run diesel buses in congested areas and inside garages.

We don't forget because we can't.

Mary had lost her father 22 years before. He was dying as Anthony was practically just beginning his job at MaBSTOA. Our loses were so many years apart, but we had the same story, and anywhere in the country that had major urbanized diesel transportation would also have survivors just like us, who know what happened to their loved ones.

"I just won the first compensation lawsuit in the country regarding diesel and cancer." I said. As I said it, I didn't know how she would take it.

"Oh my God, I can't wait to go home to tell my family about it."

She talked with some satisfaction in her voice. I had known for some time that I wasn't alone; now here was more proof.

A guy sitting next to Mary knew about the trolley garages as well. He then piped up, "Yeah the trolley garages, they were the worst. They had no ventilation at all. It's all from when the petroleum companies made a deal and put the diesel buses on the streets and didn't pay too much attention to ventilation. If the garages had ventilation at all, then it wasn't always working. Sometimes it worked, and sometimes they didn't change filters. All these people for 80 years were dying." He stopped at that point, but added, almost as an afterthought, "It might be a good idea to start a class action lawsuit. Have you ever heard the name Peter Angelos?"

"It rings a bell, but I don't know."

"Angelos used to be a big lawyer with asbestos. Forty years ago he was involved in asbestos lawsuits, and against Philip Morris, and Fan-Fan pills. Why don't you call him?"

I wrote his name down on a napkin and put it where I knew I wouldn't lose it.

My next step was to contact Peter Angelos. After the reunion, his name stayed in my head for a couple of weeks. I didn't do anything about it at first, but all that had happened at the reunion kept nagging at me.

There was a great crime committed against the people in this country, starting with the removal of the trolley cars and infrastructure decades ago. I felt in my heart that the truth had to be told.

This went far beyond Anthony and me.

It's about all the sons, husbands, fathers, and brothers who lost their lives to cancer or other diesel-related illnesses. The truth is the truth and can't be changed no matter how much money is behind the lie. It can be hidden for a long time, but eventually the facts of what happened will surface and those who were involved in tearing out vital infrastructure and exchanging it with diesel buses, while cynically calling it "progress," will be remembered in history as a watchword for greed, and corruption, and treason.

MTA management could not have remained ignorant for so many years of the effects of the diesel fumes, but money meant more to them than the lives of innocent mechanics, sweepers, bus drivers, children and people who lived in the vicinity of those depots. I had to do something.

It was November before I searched the internet for Peter Angelos. I learned that he had 10 or 15 law offices. I also found out that he owned the Baltimore Orioles. It occurred to me shortly after that he probably lived near his team, so when I eventually got enough nerve to call, I chose the number of his Baltimore office.

I got the secretary on the phone. "My name is Dorota Nigro," I said, "I won the first compensation lawsuit in the country linking diesel fumes to cancer. I'm interested in bringing a class action lawsuit."

She put me on hold. About two minutes later a lawyer got on the phone. I spoke to him for five or ten minutes and told him what I went through and that I was interested in a class action with a larger firm, one that had experience in this area, as they had with asbestos.

He listened to me, and when I was finished, he asked me a question that no one until that point had asked, "Did you do an autopsy on your husband."

"I can't believe you're the first lawyer who asked me that. Yes, I did a partial autopsy and I have partially tested it. It shows a focal accumulation of mixed dust in the macrophages with the scaring of lung tissue."

They couldn't do the tests any further in the Syracuse lab where I had them tested initially because they didn't have the equipment, and when I brought the matter up with Grey and Grey they didn't want me to pursue it any further while the case was under way.

I then told the lawyer that further tests could be done. He responded that if those cancer cell tissues showed carbon then I would have the largest lawsuit in the country. I told him that I wasn't interested in the largest lawsuit. "I'm looking to open a class action lawsuit. I'd like as many people involved because it concerns everybody, not only me."

"Doing that would take a lot of time and money," he said.

"Well, why do you think I am calling your boss's office? I have the time and he's got the money. I believe we are a perfect match."

He chuckled at that, then he asked me to send him some information and promised to respond.

I waited for a while for his response, but I didn't get one. I was just about to call them but Christmas arrived, and I figured I would give them a little more time.

I gave them a call after Christmas, but they still didn't have an answer. By then, we were getting ready to take a trip to Maui. Marriot offered me five nights at a very low rate for a time share. I had to listen to their speech to sell me on it, but the cheap price was worth hearing them talk.

Going to Maui gave us the opportunity to spread Anthony's ashes. It would also, unexpectedly, give me another reason to continue fighting.

Mary came along with us for the trip. Getting Anthony's remains there proved a little tricky and entailed going through our neighbor's daughter, Kimberly, who was a funeral director. She came and removed the ashes from the box and put them in a biodegradable plastic envelope, which floats for a little while in water but eventually sinks slowly. Because the ashes are a powder, I had some worries about getting them onto the plane. But we got through security and onto the plane with little trouble.

The grounds of the hotel in Maui were beautiful. The place was located right on the beach, and we enjoyed walking along the shore every morning and having coffee by the pool. Michael and Samantha took numerous excursions. They went zip lining with Mary. We attended a luau at the Hilton hotel, but the outing that we enjoyed the most was watching the sunrise on top of the inactive volcano.

Our main reason for coming to Maui was to put Anthony's ashes in the ocean. He loved the ocean, boating, fishing and anything that had to do with the water, so we immediately began looking for somewhere to inter him in the water. I first considered hiring a boat to take his remains out to sea, until Mary and I left the Marriott one afternoon and walked down the line of hotels on the waterfront. We walked to the end of the sand where the rocks began. It was a lovely location, and as we sat having drinks we watched Hawaiians, working for the hotel, dressed in grass skirts climb up a path and onto the cliffs carrying torches. We stopped at the restaurant there and talked about what we were going to do. Mary said, "This is a perfect place," and pointed to the cliffs.

I agreed but the trouble was getting up onto the bluffs as the entrance was blocked. We scouted for a way up, until we found a little gate, "Private" of course, which led to a path and up onto the massive rocks that opened onto a secluded bay.

After that, we went back to our own hotel, and found Michael and Samantha. We told them about what we had found and agreed to have, for lack of a better word, a ceremony, the following day as the sun set.

We returned with Michael and Samantha just before dusk the next day, and quietly entered through the gate and headed up onto the tiny path which led onto the cliff through bushes and jagged rock outcrops. Once you got up there, it was absolutely breathtaking. We carried the flower wreaths called lei with us. Sam filmed the whole thing on a Go Pro. I held Anthony's ashes in the biodegradable envelope.

The small bay below was rough and secluded. You can't swim there because of the rocks and waves, and boats don't go in there for the same reason. After a few minutes, we arrived at a perfect place for the ceremony, and, just as the sun was setting, we dropped his ashes into the water below with the flowers. The envelope floated for a while, and then turned sidewise and sank.

The sun set in the distance, sailboats passed by on the warm breeze. The memory of that day is very special to us. I am sure that if Anthony was watching from above he would approve the location, which became his final resting place.

There was solemnity in what we did, and closure, and it felt fitting for Anthony to be "buried" at sea, which he loved so much.

I remember as we left, I turned to the kids and said, "If I die of an illness that takes several months, I'll schedule a vacation here instead of a funeral. But if I go all of a sudden, you're out of luck." I laughed.

Sam filmed it and edited the ceremony over one of Anthony's favorite songs, *What a Wonderful World,* by Luis Armstrong. At first I didn't show my mother-in-law the video; I thought the memory was too fresh for that. But I eventually did. When she came to my house one day I asked her if she wanted to watch, and she agreed. She didn't cry at the table, but she left soon after, and I have a suspicion that she held her tears for the car ride home.

If our trip to Maui had been eventful by bringing us a sense of closure, the plane ride home, coincidentally or not, would again remind me of what had happened to my husband and why he had died. We flew standby, because I work for the airline. Michael had returned home the day before and we got the last three seats on the next flight out to San Francisco, but we were scattered throughout the plane. I was used to it however, and anyone who flew with me was always prepared to take whatever seat they could get on the flight.

As it turned out, I got a good window seat. I was beside a lady who was traveling with her daughter, but the two were separated. The mother was in the middle seat, and her daughter was on the other side of the aisle. It's a five-hour flight from Maui to San Francisco, where we were taking a connecting flight to New York. When I realized that she and her daughter were apart, I offered to switch seats. They gratefully accepted.

That's when I ended up beside a gentleman traveling for business. He started a conversation with me because he thought that I looked nervous.

"You seem like you're having trouble relaxing."

"I'm very antsy." I said, "I usually work while I'm on a plane. I find the time goes faster when you're working."

From there he became interested and we started talking. I realized he was a businessman, and it turned out that his business, oddly enough, was in heavy equipment, which consumed a lot of diesel, and so I understood that he knew a thing or two about diesel and its fumes. I told him about our trip to Maui.

"Where's your husband?"

I explained that we had gone to Maui to spread Anthony's ashes.

"Can I ask you what happened?"

"Yes," because he dealt with heavy equipment, I decided to explain the events in more detail. I said, "My husband passed away two-and-a-half years ago. He worked for the MTA and he died from cancer that he got from the diesel fumes he inhaled at work. I pursued the case and won. I'm also trying to open a class action lawsuit; something bigger, because this has been going on for a long time and nothing's been done about it. But I don't know exactly what to do next."

At that point, I recounted my discussion with the attorney from Peter Angelos' Baltimore office. "I wish I could help," he said and thought for a moment. "Let me give you the name of someone who might be able to help. He's my friend. His name is Alan Schaeffer. He's been researching diesel for 25-30 years." He paused and added, "Among other things he served on an advisory committee to the EPA regarding diesel. He might be a good person to talk to."

I was speechless when he said that. What were my chances of sitting next to the man whose friend works with diesel, and had been before the EPA?

We said goodbye when the flight came to an end, but as we parted ways, he kept watching me as if he was trying to remember my face.

We returned to New York on the 6th or 7th of January. I waited a little while, and then called Peter Angelos' office to find out if they had made a decision on whether or not they wanted to pursue a class action suit with me. They had had two months to make up their minds.

After waiting for a few minutes on hold, the same lawyer I had spoken with when I first called got on the phone.

"Are you going to take the case," I asked?"

"No."

"Why?"

"Time and money," he said, quickly.

"I don't buy it. I have all the time in the world, and your agency has been in business for many years; time has nothing to do with it and it's not about money for me, it's about winning. As far as money goes, I think your boss can afford it, and you know there's a case here. Everybody knows it." He started talking, but I continued, "I think you're afraid to go against petroleum companies. They work together with the government and you're scared."

"I'm sorry, we can't do it," he said.

Getting rebuffed by Peter Angelos' office gave me the motivation to call Alan Schaeffer. I thought that since I had been turned away on one avenue, another would open for me. Boy, was I wrong.

I found his office number by searching him on the internet. When I phoned, I got an assistant on the line, and left a message, telling her my name, and that I had recently been featured in the Wall Street Journal. The assistant told me that Mr. Schaeffer would return my call as soon as possible. I didn't think I had much chance of hearing from him. He was a busy man, after all. But, to my surprise, he called me back thirty minutes later. After he introduced himself, I told him about the trolley garages and the dangers of diesel and all that I knew about how people had been dying for years.

From there, I asked him for help.

When I paused, he replied, "No comment on that."

I couldn't believe what I was hearing. I never expected him to respond that way, like he didn't have to talk to me.

Despite being handled this way, I asked if he could at least send me in the right direction, after all, he had been working in this field for a very long time, he had to have known someone who could help me.

"No comment on that," he said again.

If that was his response, then why did he even bother to call me back? He knew who I was, I explained it to his assistant. At that moment, I thanked him for returning my call and wished him well.

As I was about to hang up I said, "I hope we meet one day." He didn't respond and I hung up. I felt that what I had to say about him would be better delivered in person.

When I got off the phone I was fuming mad. "Do you think I'm an idiot? I'm a woman with an accent and you just dismiss me like I'm nobody. No comment? You can't help me. Like I'm a crazy person." I said this out loud in my living room. I'm glad no one was there to hear me. But I also felt like I had failed. Like it was all over, even though it was clear how criminal the behavior of the MTA and the responsible corporations had been, there was nothing I could do.

I had to call somebody at that point. I got on the phone and dialed John Dearie. Thank God he took the call.

"John this is unacceptable," I said. "How dare the diesel guy talk to me like that. He has the audacity to tell me 'no comment,' and Peter Angelo won't take the case, and I know they have the money, and they know we have a case. I can't accept this!" I was shouting at this point and John stopped me.

"Dorota," he said, "Do you realize what you're touching? This is the biggest thing in the country."

"It's unacceptable. Whose side are you on?"

"Dorota, I tried. I lost a ton of money."

"Maybe you can do something without worrying about the money sometime," I said. I was being a little unfair to him. After all, he had taken the time and money and lost a big case. Or lost "big league" as Trump might say.

"You can't win this, Dorota. You've got to focus on something else. This won't get you anywhere. The cards are all stacked against you."

"Fine, then maybe I'm going to put it in a book." I said.

"What's it going to be a lovey dovey romance," John said with his tongue in his cheek.

"That's not funny, John. And maybe I am going to write a book that's going to be lovey dovey. I just have to vent. I have to get it out to people."

"Then I give you all the support and good luck in the world," he said and paused; then he added, "You know, you remind me of someone."

"Who's that?"

"I don't know. I have to think about it."

We talked for a bit more, and then he wished me well and we hung up. A few minutes later I got an email from his secretary Linda that said: "You remind me of Helen Reddy and the song, "I am Woman." He sent along a link to the song. I clicked on it but I couldn't hear the music. They sent me back a copy of the lyrics. "I am woman, hear me roar / In numbers too big to ignore / And I know too much to go back and pretend / 'Cause I've heard it all before / And I've been down there on the floor / No one's ever going to keep me down again."

I could picture John laughing in his office as he had his secretary send me those lyrics. At least he thought I was strong; at least it was a compliment. And I took heart from the fact that John saw me in such a light, because I had no intention of giving up now, and I didn't care if anyone was with me.

People all throughout the country had been affected by this, from the doctor I had met at my reunion, who actually gave me a hug, to Mary, who lost her father, to all of my husband's co-workers who died, this thing is far too widespread for me to be alone. We just have to band together and then it won't matter how many lawyers or organizations or congress people fight against us.

Diesel fumes in our air and our places of work, and the harm they have caused in the last eighty years or so is not a subject we can ignore anymore.

Too many people have died and are still dying. We can't pretend that it didn't happen.

The questions that kept repeating in my head were "What's next, what's next? What are you going to do now?"

"Write the book," I thought.

As I started thinking about what it would mean to write, I became more and more determined to succeed, and I thought of all the ways the book could help spread the word about what's been going on in diesel bus garages in New York City and all over the county, and how it's been going on just for money. I know the written word is more powerful than any class action lawsuit; it reaches more people, and that's what we have to do: reach as many people with this information as possible, until the bulk of the population understands that we were duped by powerful forces and corporations that sold dirty diesel buses over the clean and well-functioning surface railroads that little towns and cities across the fruited plain formerly operated. That such a useful utility was torn out in the name of progress, but really for profit, is a shame; the fact that the buses poisoned workers on top of it is a crime.

We are not just numbers in some accountant's statistic sheet, whose lives and deaths are dealt with like so many rounding errors or collateral damage. I'm not just a number. Anthony was not just a number. His friends and co-workers are not just a bunch of numbers; the same goes for the citizens of any city, town, or country affected by this. We're human beings, and we demand to be treated as such. Just as the Katyn massacre was eventually brought to light, so, too, will this injustice. Men and women have been dying from cancer in the garages and streets of New York City for generations from a preventable cause and it's about time the world knew it.

ABOUT THE AUTHORS

Born in a small town in Soviet occupied Poland, **Dorota Nigro** emigrated to the United States in 1972, where she graduated high school and received a BA in foreign languages from Montclair State College in New Jersey. She met her future husband, Anthony Nigro, in 1986 while he worked for the Manhattan Transportation Authority (MTA). The couple married in 1987 and bought a home on Long Island, where they had two beautiful and intelligent children. Upon retiring from the MTA in 2012, Anthony was diagnosed with stage IV lung cancer, caused by the diesel fumes he was exposed to as a bus mechanic. He died in under four months. After learning that his cancer was brought on by environmental causes, Dorota resolved to fight her husband's company, even though Anthony believed she could not win against such a powerful corporation and that he was "just a number." Ultimately, Dorota won the first worker's compensation lawsuit in the country linking diesel fumes to cancer in 2014 and continues to fight to spread awareness of the harm diesel fumes have caused for generations.

Chris Moore is a graduate of Columbia University and the co-author and ghostwriter of several memoirs, including Thea Rosenbaum's *No Place for a Lady*; and was editor and researcher for Abrashe

Szabrinski's memoir, *Dare to Live*, written about Szabrinski's time as a Jewish partisan fighting the Nazis in the forests outside Vilna, Lithuania during WWII. He lives with his wife, three boys, and two dogs in Connecticut.